Eighth Workshop on Speech and Language Processing for Assistive Technologies (SLPAT 2019)

Minneapolis, Minnesota, USA
7 June 2019

ISBN: 978-1-5108-8771-8

Printed from e-media with permission by:

Curran Associates, Inc.
57 Morehouse Lane
Red Hook, NY 12571

Some format issues inherent in the e-media version may also appear in this print version.

Printed by Curran Associates, Inc. (2019)

Association for Computational Linguistics
209 N. Eighth Street
Stroudsburg, Pennsylvania 18360

Phone: 1-570-476-8006
Fax: 1-570-476-0860

acl@aclweb.org

Additional copies of this publication are available from:

Curran Associates, Inc.
57 Morehouse Lane
Red Hook, NY 12571 USA
Phone: 845-758-0400
Fax: 845-758-2633
Email: curran@proceedings.com
Web: www.proceedings.com

NAACL HLT 2019

The 2019 Workshop on Speech and Language Processing for Assistive Technologies

Proceedings of the Eighth Workshop

June 7, 2019
Minneapolis, Minnesota, USA

Introduction

We are pleased to bring you the Proceedings of the 8th Workshop on Speech and Language Processing for Assistive Technologies (SLPAT), held in Minneapolis, Minnesota, USA, on June 7, 2019. This workshop was intended to bring researchers from all areas of speech and language technology with a common interest in making everyday life more accessible for people facing physical, cognitive, sensory, emotional or developmental communication challenges. This workshop builds on seven previous such workshops co-located with conferences such as ACL, NAACL, EMNLP and Interspeech. It provides an opportunity for individuals from research communities, and the individuals with whom they are working, to share research findings, and to discuss present and future challenges and the potential for collaboration and progress.

While Augmentative and Alternative Communication (AAC) is a particularly apt application area for speech and natural language processing technologies, we purposefully made the scope of the workshop broad enough to include assistive technologies (AT) as a whole, even those falling outside of AAC. Thus we have aimed at broad inclusivity, which is also manifest in the diversity of our program committee.

We thank all the people who made this event possible including both the authors and the members of the program committee.

Heidi Christensen, Kristy Hollingshead, Emily Prud'hommeaux, Frank Rudzicz, and Keith Vertanen
Co-organizers of SLPAT 2019

Organizers:

Heidi Christensen, University of Sheffield
Kristy Hollingshead, Florida Institute for Human and Machine Cognition
Emily Prud'hommeaux, Boston College
Frank Rudzicz, University of Toronto
Keith Vertanen, Michigan Technological University

Program Committee:

Jan Alexandersson, Deutsches Forschungszentrum für Künstliche Intelligenz
Cecilia Ovesdotter Alm, Rochester Institute of Technology
John Arnott, University of Dundee
Melanie Baljko, York University
Susana Bautista, Universidad Francisco de Vitoria
Yacine Bellik, LIMSI - CNRS, University Paris-Sud
Rolf Black, University of Dundee
Annelies Braffort, LIMSI, CNRS, Université Paris-Saclay
Corneliu Burileanu, University Politehnica of Bucharest
Stuart Cunningham, The University of Sheffield
Sarah Ebling, University of Zurich
Andrew Fowler, Google
Thomas Francois, Université catholique de Louvain
Kathleen Fraser, National Research Council Canada
Corinne Fredouille, CERI/LIA - University of Avignon
Björn Granström, KTH Royal Institute of Technology
Mark Hasegawa-Johnson, University of Illinois at Urbana-Champaign
Mark Hawley, The University of Sheffield
Graeme Hirst, University of Toronto
Matt Huenerfauth, Rochester Institute of Technology
Simon Judge, Barnsley AT Team
Per Ola Kristensson, University of Cambridge
Javier Latorre, Amazon
Benjamin Lecouteux, Laboratoire Informatique de Grenoble
William Li, Apple Inc. (Siri)
Peter Ljunglöf, Chalmers and University of Gothenburg
Eduardo Lleida, University of Zaragoza
Ornella Mich, Fondazione Bruno Kessler
Ibrahim Missaoui, ENIT
Vigouroux Nadine, IRIT
Yael Netzer, Ben Gurion University
François Portet, Université Grenoble Alpes
Emanuele Principi, Università Politecnica delle Marche
Sriranjani Ramakrishnan, Indian Institute of Technology Madras
Joseph Reddington, Royal Holloway
Ehud Reiter, University of Aberdeen
Masoud Rouhizadeh, Johns Hopkins University
Michel Vacher, Laboratoire LIG, équipe GETALP
Jun Wang, The University of Texas at Dallas

Table of Contents

Workshop Program

Friday, June 7, 2019

9:00–9:30	*Opening Remarks*
9:30–10:00	*A user study to compare two conversational assistants designed for people with hearing impairments* Anja Virkkunen, Juri Lukkarila, Kalle Palomäki and Mikko Kurimo
10:00–10:30	*Modeling Acoustic-Prosodic Cues for Word Importance Prediction in Spoken Dialogues* Sushant Kafle, Cissi Ovesdotter Alm and Matt Huenerfauth
10:30–11:00	*Break*
11:00–11:30	*Permanent Magnetic Articulograph (PMA) vs Electromagnetic Articulograph (EMA) in Articulation-to-Speech Synthesis for Silent Speech Interface* Beiming Cao, Nordine Sebkhi, Ted Mau, Omer T Inan and Jun Wang
11:30–12:00	*Speech-based Estimation of Bulbar Regression in Amyotrophic Lateral Sclerosis* Alan Wisler, Kristin Teplansky, Jordan Green, Yana Yunusova, Thomas Campbell, Daragh Heitzman and Jun Wang
12:00–14:00	*Lunch*
14:00–14:30	*A Blissymbolics Translation System* Usman Sohail and David Traum
14:30–15:00	*Investigating Speech Recognition for Improving Predictive AAC* Jiban Adhikary, Robbie Watling, Crystal Fletcher, Alex Stanage and Keith Vertanen
15:00–15:30	*Break*
15:30–16:00	*Noisy Neural Language Modeling for Typing Prediction in BCI Communication* Rui Dong, David Smith, Shiran Dudy and Steven Bedrick
16:00–16:15	*Closing Remarks*

A user study to compare two conversational assistants designed for people with hearing impairments

Anja Virkkunen
Aalto University, Finland
anja.virkkunen@aalto.fi

Juri Lukkarila
Aalto University, Finland
juri.lukkarila@aalto.fi

Kalle Palomäki
Aalto University, Finland
kalle.palomaki@aalto.fi

Mikko Kurimo
Aalto University, Finland
mikko.kurimo@aalto.fi

Abstract

Participating in conversations can be difficult for people with hearing loss, especially in acoustically challenging environments. We studied the preferences the hearing impaired have for a personal conversation assistant based on automatic speech recognition (ASR) technology. We created two prototypes which were evaluated by hearing impaired test users. This paper qualitatively compares the two based on the feedback obtained from the tests. The first prototype was a proof-of-concept system running real-time ASR on a laptop. The second prototype was developed for a mobile device with the recognizer running on a separate server. In the mobile device, augmented reality (AR) was used to help the hearing impaired observe gestures and lip movements of the speaker simultaneously with the transcriptions. Several testers found the systems useful enough to use in their daily lives, with majority preferring the mobile AR version. The biggest concern of the testers was the accuracy of the transcriptions and the lack of speaker identification.

1 Introduction

Hearing loss can make the participation in normal conversations an exhausting task, because people with hearing impairments need to focus more on the conversation to be able to keep up (Arlinger, 2003). This can cause the deaf and hard of hearing to withdraw from social interactions, leading to isolation and poorer well-being (Arlinger, 2003). Having access to an automatic speech recognizer (ASR) designed to answer their needs could make participation in everyday conversations considerably easier for them.

People with hearing impairment are a heterogeneous group with significant variability in the degree of hearing loss and its causes. Hearing aids and implants can restore hearing to a degree, but they struggle in noisy environments (Goehring et al., 2016). Many people with hearing impairments also refuse to use aids because they are perceived as uncomfortable or costly (Gates and Mills, 2005). Professional human interpreters can help the deaf and hard of hearing with their near real-time transcription, but they require advance booking and are also costly (Lasecki et al., 2017).

ASR has the potential to both function as a support and a replacement to other solutions. The strengths of ASR include accessibility with little cost, nearly real-time transcription and independence of costly human labour. Furthermore, it can be helpful to anyone irrespective of their degree of hearing loss. The weaknesses of ASR are in robustness and the lack of support for speaker diarization. And even though the accuracy of ASR has improved to a level where it rivals human transcribers (Xiong et al., 2017), noisy environments, accented speakers, and far-field microphones remain a challenge (Yu and Deng, 2015). Additionally, recognizing and conveying paralinguistic features like tone, pitch and gestures is difficult for automatic systems.

The objective of our work is to study the preferences of the deaf and hard of hearing when using ASR-based conversation assistants. We constructed two pilot Finnish language ASR systems for two portable devices with different display options. The first system is a standalone laptop ASR that does not utilize network connection or video camera. The second system is a mobile device wirelessly connected to an ASR server. In the mobile device the ASR transcript is shown in augmented video stream next to the head of the speaker. The purpose of this augmented reality

Proceedings of the Eighth Workshop on Speech and Language Processing for Assistive Technologies, pages 1–8
Minneapolis, Minnesota, USA ©2019 Association for Computational Linguistics

(AR) view is to reduce visual dispersion, which in this case refers to the need of the user to switch attention between multiple visuals. These two setups were tested by deaf and hard of hearing users, who were then interviewed to find out their preferences. We review the results and compare the feedback the systems received.

1.1 Previous work

Automatic speech recognition research focusing specifically on helping people with hearing impairments has gone on at least since 1996 (Robison and Jensema, 1996). The first assistive ASR system for the Finnish deaf and hard of hearing was devised in 1997 (Karjalainen et al., 1997). Since then, helping the deaf and hard of hearing in their school environment has been a concern in many assistive ASR systems. A lot of this research focuses in providing real-time ASR-generated transcriptions of lectures (Wald, 2006; Kheir and Way, 2007; Ranchal et al., 2013). Major effort is also dedicated to improving the ASR aided learning experience in other ways, such as minimizing visual dispersion (Cavender et al., 2009; Kushalnagar and Kushalnagar, 2014; Kushalnagar et al., 2010), comparing captioning and transcribing of online video lectures (Kushalnagar et al., 2013), and using human editors to correct ASR output (Wald, 2006). Our work focuses more generally on helping people with hearing impairments in conversational situations, not just the school setting.

Other notable applications include the system of Matthews et al. (2006), where mobile phones were used for delivering human-made transcriptions via text messages. They showed transcriptions could help people with hearing impairments, but lacked the ASR component. The transcription table design from Van Gelder et al. (2005) provided all meeting participants with partial text support. The aim there was to minimize the stigma on the deaf or hard of hearing participant.

The idea to use AR has also been introduced before in the work of Mirzaei et al. (2012, 2014) and Suemitsu et al. (2015). The system of Mirzaei et al. is similar to our mobile AR system, but it is developed for ultra mobile personal computers and has a text-to-speech component. In the work of Suemitsu et al. the focus is on reducing effect of noise with directional microphones and beamforming. As a consequence, their system works well only if the speaker is directly in front of the user. Moreover, both of these works lack the user perspective because the focus is more on the system design.

2 Conversation Assistant

Our aim in building the two Conversation Assistant systems was to provide automatic transcriptions to people with hearing impairments in a useful format. A useful conversation assistant system can (1) recognize large-vocabulary continuous speech in real-time, (2) manage varying acoustic environments with noise, and (3) present the transcriptions in a clear manner. Achieving the first two requirements is possible with modern speech recognition systems, however, their computing power and memory consumption pose limitations on the system design. The minimal solution to the third requirement would be to just display the recognition results on a screen, but looking at the screen would cause the user to miss nonverbal communication, like gestures.

We built two prototypes of the Conversation Assistant system: one running on a laptop and one on a mobile device with augmented reality (AR) capabilities. In both systems, Kaldi Speech Recognition Toolkit (Povey et al., 2011) was used to build the speech recognition models. In addition, we used Gst-Kaldi, a GStreamer plugin, for handling the incoming audio. The source codes for both the laptop version[1] and the mobile AR version[2] are published on Github.

2.1 Laptop

The laptop version was built for the first round of user tests, to find out the preferences of the deaf and hard of hearing for the Conversation Assistant concept in general. We therefore built a decidedly simple system. It ran a Kaldi speech recognition model locally on a laptop. The acoustic model of the automatic speech recognizer was a feed-forward deep neural network, trained on multi-condition data to increase noise robustness. The robustness to noise is important, because conversations are rarely had in silent environment. The data for training the acoustic model came from the SPEECON corpus (Iskra et al., 2002). The language model was trained using the *Kielipankki*[3]

[1] https://github.com/Esgrove/mastersthesis

[2] https://github.com/aalto-speech/conversation-assistant

[3] The Language Bank of Finland

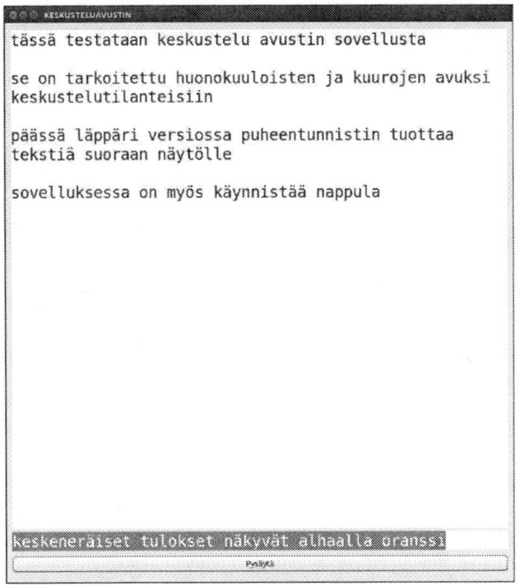

(a) Laptop version. The speech recognition results are at the top of the window. The speech being recognized currently is displayed at the bottom with orange background.

(b) Mobile AR version. The speech recognition results are placed in speech bubbles next to the face of the speaker.

Figure 1: User interface screenshots from the software.

corpus and the lexicon was based on morphs (Virpioja et al., 2013) instead of words, because of the morphological complexity of Finnish. The speech recognition model had a word error rate (WER) of 29.7 % when tested on (low-noise) broadcast news data from the Finnish public broadcaster YLE (Lukkarila, 2017). The user interface (UI), shown in Figure 1a, was kept minimal with only a record button and space for the transcription results. A more detailed description of the system is given in (Lukkarila, 2017).

2.2 Mobile AR

The main objective of the mobile AR Conversation Assistant was to move the laptop-based system to a mobile device platform and use AR to bring the transcriptions and a visual of the speaker close to each other. With the latter we aimed to reduce the amount of non-verbal communication the user loses when switching between the speaker and the transcriptions. The reduced computational capabilities of mobile devices necessitated splitting the system into a separate mobile AR application and a speech recognition server.

The mobile application was developed for the iOS platform using a 10.5" iPad Pro tablet from Apple as a test device. In the application, AR camera is used to provide a view of the speaker. The face of the speaker is located locally on the device with a face recognition algorithm provided as part of iOS toolkits. When speech is recorded by the device, the application sends the audio to the server for recognition. The text transcriptions returned from the server are then placed in speech bubbles next to the detected face as shown in Figure 1b. The bubbles follow the face of the speaker, if he or she moves in the screen.

The server side uses an open-source Kaldi Server implementation (Alumäe, 2014) based on Gst-Kaldi. The server is split to a controlling master server unit and workers responsible for the recognition process. Each mobile device connecting to the server needs one worker to do the transcribing and connections between the two are handled by the master server. The master server and the workers can be run on different machines and all the communication happens over the internet. This requires stable connections from all parties, including the mobile client, but on the upside, the system can be scaled up as much as needed.

In the speech recognizer, the acoustic model was a combination of time-delay and long short-term memory neural network trained with Finnish Parliament Speech Corpus (Mansikkaniemi et al., 2017). This training data is significantly larger than the one used for the laptop system, but includes little background noise. The language model was trained with the same data as in the laptop system, but utilizing a more recent subword modeling optimized for Kaldi's weighted finite state transducer architecture (Smit et al., 2017). The speech recognition model scored WER of 18.56 % on the YLE data which is more than a 10 % absolute improvement over the model in the laptop system (Mansikkaniemi et al., 2017). Even though these evaluations were not performed for noisy tasks, we expect that the improvement is substantial enough to cover the lack of noise-robustness for our user tests. For a more detailed description of the system, see the work in (Virkkunen, 2018).

3 User tests

To evaluate the prototypes, we organized user tests for both versions with deaf and hard of hearing participants. Our aim was to simulate noisy conversational situations to see how much the Conversation Assistant could help the tester in following the conversation. In the user tests of the laptop version, the participant had a conversation with and without the support of the Conversation Assistant. In the mobile AR tests, the comparison was made between a text-only view similar to the laptop version and the AR view seen in figure 1b. The contents of this section are further detailed in (Lukkarila, 2017) and (Virkkunen, 2018).

The test users were recruited with the help of *Kuuloliitto*, the association of the deaf and hard of hearing in Finland. The number of participants for the laptop and mobile AR versions were nine and twelve, respectively. The sample size was limited by the number of volunteers we were able to find. Each participant was also asked to give a written consent and permission to record the test session. Six people took part in both tests so in total there were 15 unique participants. The age of the testers, excluding two who refused to disclose their age, ranged from 15 to 84, with the median age being 55. All except two participants were women. Two of the participants were deaf, but they could communicate verbally. The rest had different degrees of hearing loss and used either hearing aids, cochlear implants or both in their daily lives. Four participants also had used ASR applications before, for example personal voice assistants, automatic video captioning, the Google Translate service and note takers.

3.1 Test setup

The test setup simulated a conversation of two people in a noisy environment. The test administrator and the participant would sit face-to-face at a table surrounded by loudspeakers playing a looped noise recording from a busy cafe. The participant had the laptop/mobile device in front of them and they could freely alternate between following the application and their conversation partner. In the case of mobile AR, the participant could choose to hold the device in their hands or place it on a tripod. The test was designed to last for one hour and the feedback was collected using a questionnaire. The overall structure and content of the questionnaires is the same between the two user tests, but small changes were made to the mobile AR version to reflect the changes in the system.

The test and the questionnaire had four sections: introduction, word explaining, conversation, and debriefing. In the introduction the test participant was familiarized with the test plan and the Conversation Assistant. The participant was also asked to fill in their background information in the questionnaire. In the debriefing section, the participant was asked to give overall feedback on the system.

The first task, word explaining, consisted of the test administrator explaining words from a list to the participant, who tried to guess the word in question. Halfway through the task, the participant was asked to switch between the compared methods (without versus with Conversation Assistant or text view versus AR view). After finishing the word list or running out of time, the participant gave feedback in the questionnaire. In the second task, the conversation, the test administrator conversed with the test participant on a range of common topics from hobbies to food and travel for 10-15 minutes. Switch between the compared methods was made at the midpoint again. And after a time limit set for the task was reached, the participant was asked to give feedback on the questionnaire.

3.2 Results

The questionnaire had questions with both written and numeric format. Question with written feedback were concerned with the potential use cases of the system and its strengths and weaknesses. The numeric questions assessed the perceived quality of the system and the preferences of the testers. The numeric questions further break

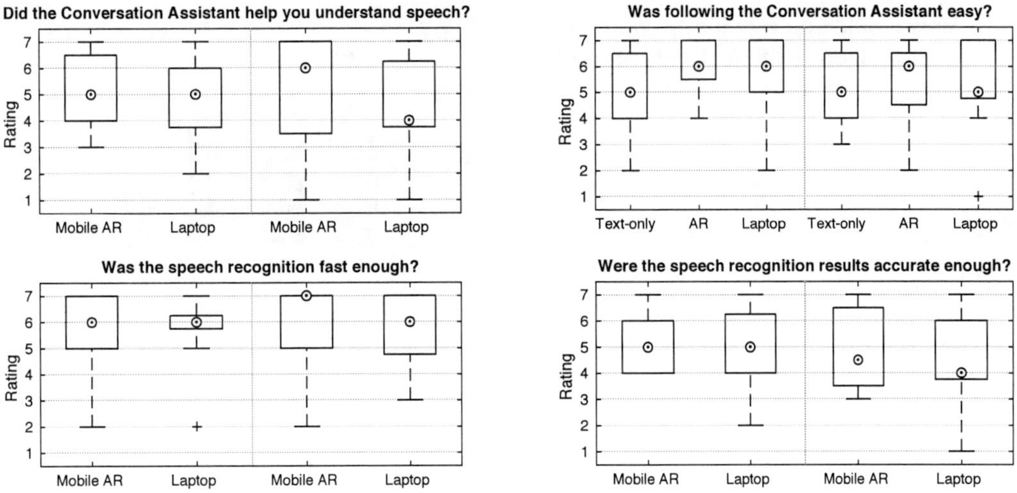

Figure 2: Rating results from task 1, word explanation (left side of each plot) and task 2, conversation (right side of each plot). The range from one to seven is the same as in Figure 3.

down into binary choices, one multiple-choice question and rating questions. The rating questions had a range from one (negative) to seven (positive). Questions with numeric format also had text fields where the testers could elaborate their choices if they wanted.

Several numeric results (Table 1, Figure 3 and top-left of Figure 2) show that the participants found both Conversation Assistant systems useful. Majority of the participants would adopt a Conversation Assistant system in their daily lives. Potential use cases and environments mentioned included daily conversations, meetings, museums, restaurants, live television, lectures and office. Speed and ease of following the output in both systems were also rated favorably with few exceptions in Figure 2. Those who disagreed said that the following suffered mostly from recognition errors. Another point raised was the movement and positioning of the speech bubbles in the mobile AR version which felt distracting to some.

Speech recognition errors were the biggest problem reducing the perceived utility of the sys-

Would you use an application like the Conversation Assistant in your daily life?	
Yes: 83 %	No: 17 %
Which mode would you prefer?	
With AR view: 67 %	Text-only view: 33 %
Which one of the following options is better?	
Text appears faster (<1 sec), but contains more mistakes: 67 %	Text appears slower (>1 sec), but contains less mistakes: 33 %

Table 1: Results to the binary questions asked in the user tests of the mobile AR version.

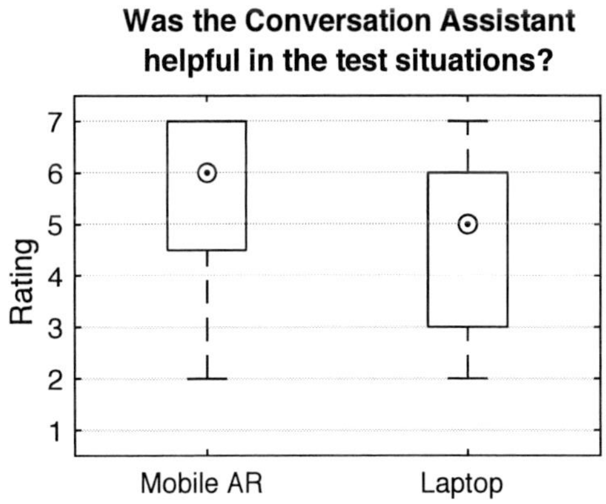

Figure 3: Rating of the overall usefulness of the system. The range is from one (negative) to seven (positive). In the box plots, the circle with the dot marks the median. The bottom and top of the box correspond to 25th and 75th percentiles, respectively. The sample is skewed if the median is not at the middle of the box. The whiskers show the extreme data points that are not considered outliers. The data points outside the whiskers are marked with plus signs.

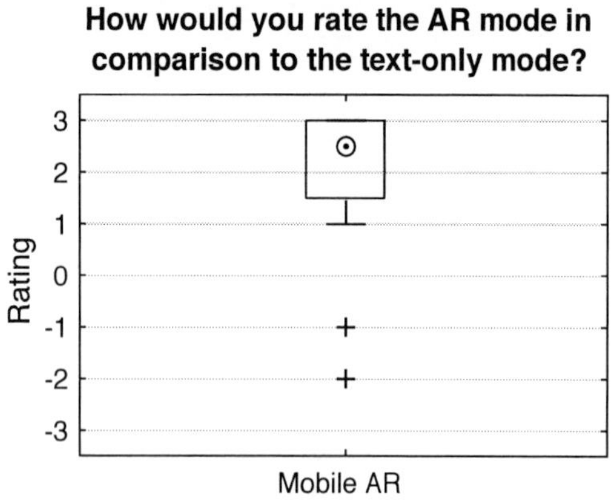

Figure 4: In the user tests of the mobile AR version, the testers were asked to rate whether they preferred having AR view over the text-only view. The range is from minus three (much worse) to three (much better).

tem. The ratings are similar for the two systems, but the AR mobile has less negative ratings overall. In Figure 2 it can be seen that ratings of the accuracy reflect the ratings of the helpfulness. Many felt the transcriptions helped them get an idea of the conversation, but that they could not solely rely on the transcriptions because of the errors. Moreover, a couple of participants noted they used the Conversation Assistant only a little because they could use lip reading instead. They would need transcriptions only in group conversations or in cases where the face of the speaker cannot be seen.

Figure 4 shows that the user testers preferred the AR view over having text-only view similar to the laptop version. Majority of the answers cited the ability to use lip reading in AR view as the decisive factor. Two participants thought the views would have different use cases, for example the text-only view could be useful in meetings. One found the text-only view cleaner and easier to follow than the AR view. Some testers also worried that pointing the device camera at the conversation partner in the mobile AR version would feel inappropriate.

Figure 5 shows the participants preferences for end-user devices. It is clear from the answers that the device needs to be mobile to be of any use. Most people would like to have the application on their smartphones, as it is a device most people own and carry around everywhere. Tablets and laptops also get many votes, especially from working age people. Smart glasses got votes from three curious participants, though we anticipated more. We hypothesize the image most people have of

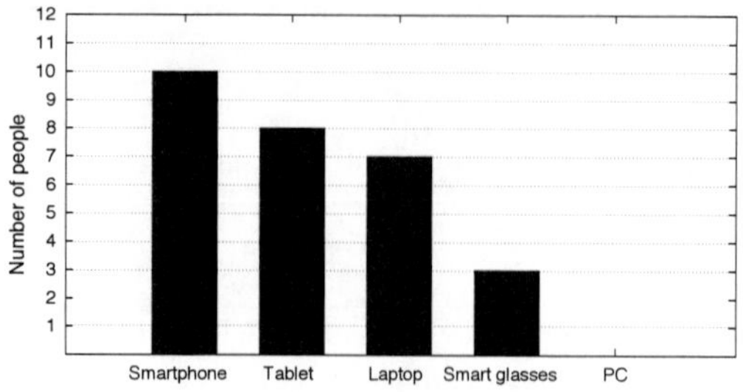

Figure 5: Which device the participants would like to use the Conversation Assistant on.

AR glasses is that they are bulky, impractical and stand out. This could explain the lack of appeal the glasses had among the participants.

4 Conclusions

We evaluated two prototypes of a conversational assistant for the deaf and hard of hearing by user tests. The results show that it is already possible to build an assistive application the deaf and hard of hearing find useful with current technology. In the written feedback many expressed the urgent need for this type of application. Several people noted they would download the mobile application if it were available, despite its flaws. Majority of the test users preferred the mobile AR version because it supported their use of lip reading. A couple of participants saw potential use for both versions depending on the situation.

Accuracy of the transcriptions was the biggest issue in need of improvement according to the participants. Several testers also noted that group conversations in noise are the most difficult to follow. For them, speaker diarization would be the feature that would make the Conversation Assistant truly useful. Both systems also lack direct unmediated eye contact which could be potentially solved with AR glasses. However, to be widely adopted, the glasses would have to be unobtrusive and light weight.

Acknowledgments

This work was funded by the Academy of Finland as part of the project "Conversation assistant for the hearing impaired" (305503) and Kone Foundation. The writers would also like to thank Katri Leino, Tanel Alumäe and Kuuloliitto for help and resources.

References

Tanel Alumäe. 2014. Full-duplex speech-to-text system for estonian. In *Baltic HLT 2014*, pages 3–10, Kaunas, Lithuania.

Stig Arlinger. 2003. Negative consequences of uncorrected hearing loss-a review. *International journal of audiology*, 42:2S17–2S20.

Anna C Cavender, Jeffrey P Bigham, and Richard E Ladner. 2009. Classinfocus: enabling improved visual attention strategies for deaf and hard of hearing students. In *Proceedings of the 11th international ACM SIGACCESS conference on Computers and accessibility*, pages 67–74. ACM.

George A Gates and John H Mills. 2005. Presbycusis. *The Lancet*, 366(9491):1111–1120.

Tobias Goehring, Xin Yang, Jessica JM Monaghan, and Stefan Bleeck. 2016. Speech enhancement for hearing-impaired listeners using deep neural networks with auditory-model based features. In *2016 24th European Signal Processing Conference (EUSIPCO)*, pages 2300–2304.

Dorota J. Iskra, Beate Grosskopf, Krzysztof Marasek, Henk van den Heuvel, Frank Diehl, and Andreas Kiessling. 2002. Speecon - speech databases for consumer devices: Database specification and validation. In *LREC*.

Matti Karjalainen, Peter Boda, Panu Somervuo, and Toomas Altosaar. 1997. Applications for the hearing-impaired: Evaluation of Finnish phoneme recognition methods. In *Fifth European Conference on Speech Communication and Technology*.

Richard Kheir and Thomas Way. 2007. Inclusion of deaf students in computer science classes using real-time speech transcription. In *Proceedings of the 12th Annual SIGCSE Conference on Innovation and Technology in Computer Science Education*, ITiCSE '07, pages 261–265. ACM.

Raja Kushalnagar and Poorna Kushalnagar. 2014. Collaborative gaze cues and replay for deaf and hard of hearing students. In *Computers Helping People with Special Needs*, pages 415–422, Cham. Springer International Publishing.

Raja S. Kushalnagar, Anna C. Cavender, and Jehan-François Pâris. 2010. Multiple view perspectives: Improving inclusiveness and video compression in mainstream classroom recordings. In *Proceedings of the 12th International ACM SIGACCESS Conference on Computers and Accessibility*, ASSETS '10, pages 123–130, New York, NY, USA. ACM.

Raja S. Kushalnagar, Walter S. Lasecki, and Jeffrey P. Bigham. 2013. Captions versus transcripts for online video content. In *Proceedings of the 10th International Cross-Disciplinary Conference on Web Accessibility*, W4A '13, pages 32:1–32:4, New York, NY, USA. ACM.

Walter S. Lasecki, Christopher D. Miller, Iftekhar Naim, Raja Kushalnagar, Adam Sadilek, Daniel Gildea, and Jeffrey P. Bigham. 2017. Scribe: Deep integration of human and machine intelligence to caption speech in real time. *Commun. ACM*, 60(9):93–100.

Juri Lukkarila. 2017. Developing a conversation assistant for the hearing impaired using automatic speech recognition. MSc Thesis, Aalto University.

André Mansikkaniemi, Peter Smit, Mikko Kurimo, et al. 2017. Automatic construction of the Finnish parliament speech corpus. In *INTERSPEECH 2017–18th Annual Conference of the International Speech Communication Association*.

Tara Matthews, Scott Carter, Carol Pai, Janette Fong, and Jennifer Mankoff. 2006. Scribe4me: Evaluating a mobile sound transcription tool for the deaf. In *UbiComp 2006: Ubiquitous Computing*, pages 159–176. Springer.

Mohammad Reza Mirzaei, Seyed Ghorshi, and Mohammad Mortazavi. 2012. Combining augmented reality and speech technologies to help deaf and hard of hearing people. In *2012 14th Symposium on Virtual and Augmented Reality*, pages 174–181.

Mohammad Reza Mirzaei, Seyed Ghorshi, and Mohammad Mortazavi. 2014. Audio-visual speech recognition techniques in augmented reality environments. *The Visual Computer*, 30(3):245–257.

Daniel Povey, Arnab Ghoshal, Gilles Boulianne, Lukas Burget, Ondrej Glembek, Nagendra Goel, Mirko Hannemann, Petr Motlicek, Yanmin Qian, Petr Schwarz, Jan Silovsky, Georg Stemmer, and Karel Vesely. 2011. The Kaldi speech recognition toolkit. In *IEEE 2011 Workshop on Automatic Speech Recognition and Understanding*. IEEE Signal Processing Society. IEEE Catalog No.: CFP11SRW-USB.

Rohit Ranchal, Teresa Taber-Doughty, Yiren Guo, Keith Bain, Heather Martin, J Paul Robinson, and Bradley S Duerstock. 2013. Using speech recognition for real-time captioning and lecture transcription in the classroom. *IEEE Transactions on Learning Technologies*, 6(4):299–311.

Joseph Robison and Carl Jensema. 1996. Computer speech recognition as an assistive device for deaf and hard of hearing people. In *Biennial Conference on Postsecondary Education for Persons Who Are Deaf or Hard of Hearing (7th, Knoxville, Tennessee*, volume 948, page 154. ERIC.

Peter Smit, Sami Virpioja, and Mikko Kurimo. 2017. Improved subword modeling for WFST-based speech recognition. In *INTERSPEECH 2017 – 18th Annual Conference of the International Speech Communication Association*, pages 2551–2555, Stockholm, Sweden.

Kazuki Suemitsu, Keiichi Zempo, Koichi Mizutani, and Naoto Wakatsuki. 2015. Caption support system for complementary dialogical information using see-through head mounted display. In *2015 IEEE 4th Global Conference on Consumer Electronics (GCCE)*, pages 368–371.

Joris Van Gelder, Irene Van Peer, and Dzmitry Aliakseyeu. 2005. Transcription table: Text support during meetings. In *IFIP Conference on Human-Computer Interaction*, pages 1002–1005. Springer.

Anja Virkkunen. 2018. Automatic speech recognition for the hearing impaired in an augmented reality application. MSc Thesis, Aalto University.

Sami Virpioja, Peter Smit, Stig-Arne Grönroos, and Mikko Kurimo. 2013. Morfessor 2.0: Python implementation and extensions for Morfessor Baseline. Technical report, Aalto University.

Mike Wald. 2006. Captioning for deaf and hard of hearing people by editing automatic speech recognition in real time. In *Computers Helping People with Special Needs*, pages 683–690, Berlin, Heidelberg. Springer.

Wayne Xiong, Jasha Droppo, Xuedong Huang, Frank Seide, Michael L Seltzer, Andreas Stolcke, Dong Yu, and Geoffrey Zweig. 2017. Toward human parity in conversational speech recognition. *IEEE/ACM Transactions on Audio, Speech and Language Processing (TASLP)*, 25(12):2410–2423.

Dong Yu and Li Deng. 2015. *Automatic Speech Recognition: A Deep Learning Approach*. Springer, London.

Modeling Acoustic-Prosodic Cues for Word Importance Prediction in Spoken Dialogues

Sushant Kafle, Cecilia O. Alm, Matt Huenerfauth
Rochester Institute of Technology, Rochester NY
{sxk5664,matt.huenerfauth,coagla}@rit.edu

Abstract

Prosodic cues in conversational speech aid listeners in discerning a message. We investigate whether acoustic cues in spoken dialogue can be used to identify the importance of individual words to the meaning of a conversation turn. Individuals who are Deaf and Hard of Hearing often rely on real-time captions in live meetings. Word error rate, a traditional metric for evaluating automatic speech recognition (ASR), fails to capture that some words are more important for a system to transcribe correctly than others. We present and evaluate neural architectures that use acoustic features for 3-class word importance prediction. Our model performs competitively against state-of-the-art text-based word-importance prediction models, and it demonstrates particular benefits when operating on imperfect ASR output.

1 Introduction

Not all words are equally important to the meaning of a spoken message. Identifying the importance of words is useful for a variety of tasks including text classification and summarization (Hong and Nenkova, 2014; Yih et al., 2007). Considering the relative importance of words can also be valuable when evaluating the quality of output of an automatic speech recognition (ASR) system for specific tasks, such as caption generation for Deaf and Hard of Hearing (DHH) participants in spoken meetings (Kafle and Huenerfauth, 2017).

As described by Berke et al. (2018), interlocutors may submit audio of individual utterances through a mobile device to a remote ASR system, with the text output appearing on an app for DHH users. With ASR being applied to new tasks such as this, it is increasingly important to evaluate ASR output effectively. Traditional Word Error Rate (WER)-based evaluation assumes that all word transcription errors equally impact the quality of the ASR output for a user. However, this is less helpful for various applications (McCowan et al., 2004; Morris et al., 2004). In particular, Kafle and Huenerfauth (2017) found that metrics with differential weighting of errors based on word importance correlate better with human judgment than WER does for the automatic captioning task. However, prior models based on text features for word importance identification (Kafle and Huenerfauth, 2018; Sheikh et al., 2016) face challenges when applied to conversational speech:

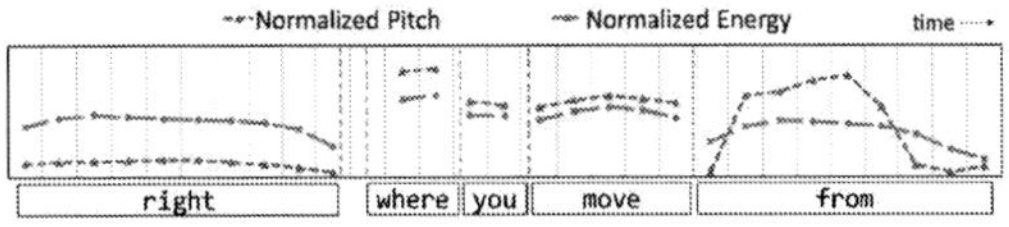

Figure 1: Example of conversational transcribed text, *right where you move from*, that is difficult to disambiguate without prosody. The intended sentence structure was: *Right! Where you move from?*

- **Difference from Formal Texts**: Unlike formal texts, conversational transcripts may lack capitalization or punctuation, use informal grammatical structures, or contain disfluencies (e.g. incomplete words or edits, hesitations, repetitions), filler words, or more frequent out-of-vocabulary (and invented) words (McKeown et al., 2005).

- **Availability and Reliability**: Text transcripts of spoken conversations require a human transcriptionist or an ASR system, but ASR transcription is not always reliable or even feasible, especially for noisy environments, nonstandard language use, or low-resource languages, etc.

While spoken messages include prosodic cues that focus a listener's attention on the most important parts of the message (Frazier et al., 2006),

Proceedings of the Eighth Workshop on Speech and Language Processing for Assistive Technologies, pages 9–16
Minneapolis, Minnesota, USA ©2019 Association for Computational Linguistics

such information may be omitted from a text transcript, as in Figure 1, in which the speaker pauses after "right" (suggesting a boundary) and uses rising intonation on "from" (suggesting a question). Moreover, there are application scenarios where transcripts of spoken messages are not always available or fully reliable. In such cases, models based on a speech signal (without a text transcript) might be preferred.

With this motivation, we investigate modeling acoustic-prosodic cues for predicting the importance of words to the meaning of a spoken dialogue. Our goal is to explore the versatility of speech-based (text-independent) features for word importance modeling. In this work, we frame the task of word importance prediction as sequence labeling and utilize a bi-directional Long Short-Term Memory (LSTM)-based neural architecture for context modeling on speech.

2 Related Work

Many researchers have considered how to identify the importance of a word and have proposed methods for this task. Popular methods include frequency-based unsupervised measures of importance, such as Term Frequency-Inverse Document Frequency (TF-IDF), and word co-occurrence measures (HaCohen-Kerner et al., 2005; Matsuo and Ishizuka, 2004), which are primarily used for extracting relevant keywords from text documents. Other supervised measures of word importance have been proposed (Liu et al., 2011, 2004; Hulth, 2003; Sheeba and Vivekanandan, 2012; Kafle and Huenerfauth, 2018) for various applications. Closest to our current work, researchers in (Kafle and Huenerfauth, 2018) described a neural network-based model for capturing the importance of a word at the sentence level. Their setup differed from traditional importance estimation strategies for document-level keyword-extraction, which had treated each *word* as a *term* in a document such that all *words* identified by a *term* received a uniform importance score, without regard to context. Similar to our application use-case, the model proposed by Kafle and Huenerfauth (2018) identified word importance at a more granular level, i.e. sentence- or utterance-level. However, their model operated on human-generated transcripts of text. Since we focus on real-time captioning applications, we prefer a model that can operate without such human-produced transcripts, as discussed in Section 1.

Previous researchers have modeled prosodic cues in speech for various applications (Tran et al., 2017; Brenier et al., 2005; Xie et al., 2009). For instance, in automatic prominence detection, researchers predict regions of speech with relatively more spoken stress (Wang and Narayanan, 2007; Brenier et al., 2005; Tamburini, 2003). Identification of prominence aids automatically identifying content words (Wang and Narayanan, 2007), a crucial sub-task of spoken language understanding (Beckman and Venditti, 2000; Mishra et al., 2012). Moreover, researchers have investigated modeling prosodic patterns in spoken messages to identify syntactic relationships among words (Price et al., 1991; Tran et al., 2017). In particular, Tran et al. demonstrated the effectiveness of speech-based features in improving the constituent parsing of conversational speech texts. In other work, researchers investigated prosodic events to identify important segments in speech, useful for producing a generic summary of the recordings of meetings (Xie et al., 2009; Murray et al., 2005). At the same time, prosodic cues are also challenging in that they serve a range of linguistic functions and convey affect. We investigate models applied to spoken messages at a dialogue-turn level, for predicting the importance of words for understanding an utterance.

3 Word Importance Prediction

For the task of word importance prediction, we formulate a sequence labeling architecture that takes as input a spoken dialogue turn utterance with word-level timestamps[1], and assigns an importance label to every spoken word in the turn using a bi-directional LSTM architecture (Huang et al., 2015; Lample et al., 2016).

$$\overrightarrow{h_t} = LSTM(s_t, \overrightarrow{h_{t-1}}) \tag{1}$$

$$\overleftarrow{h_t} = LSTM(s_t, \overleftarrow{h_{t-1}}) \tag{2}$$

The word-level timestamp information is used to generate an acoustic-prosodic representation for each word (s_t) from the speech signal. Two LSTM units, moving in opposite directions through these

[1]For the purposes of accurately evaluating efficacy of speech-based feature for word importance, we currently make use of high-quality human-annotated word-level timestamp information in our train/evaluation corpus; in the future, speech tokenization could be automated.

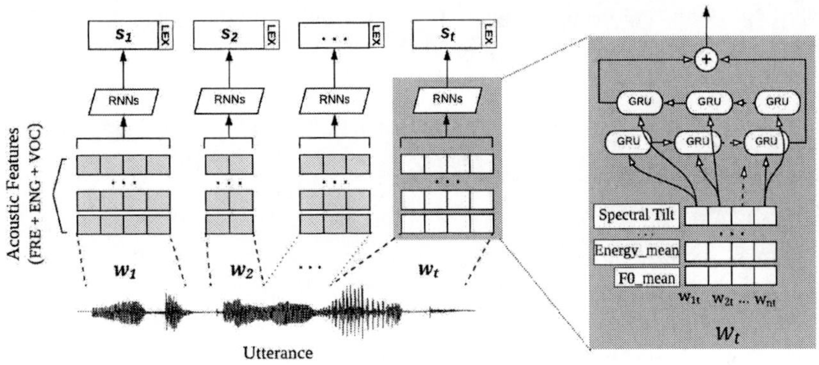

Figure 2: Architecture for feature representation of spoken words using time series speech data. For each spoken word (w) identified by a word-level timestamp, a fixed-length interval window (τ) slides through to get $n = time(w)/\tau$ sub-word interval segments. Using an RNN network, a word-level feature (s), represented by a fixed-length vector, is extracted using the features from a variable-length sub-word sequence.

word units (s_t) in an utterance, are then used for constructing a context-aware representation for every word. Each LSTM unit takes as input the representation of the word (s_t), along with the hidden state from the previous time step, and each outputs a new hidden state. At each time step, the hidden representations from both LSTMs are concatenated $h_t = [\overrightarrow{h_t}; \overleftarrow{h_t}]$, in order to obtain a contextualized representation for each word. This representation is next passed through a projection layer (details below) to the final prediction for a word.

3.1 Importance as Ordinal Classification

We define word importance prediction as the task of classifying the words into one of the many importance classes, e.g., high importance (HI), medium importance (MID) and low importance (LOW) (details on Section 5). These importance class labels have a natural *ordering* such that the cost of misclassification is not uniform e.g., incorrect classification of HI class for LI class (or vice-versa) will have higher error cost than classification of HI class for MI. Considering this ordinal nature of the importance class labels, we investigate three different projection layers for output prediction: a softmax layer for making local importance prediction (SOFTMAX), a relaxed softmax tailored for ordinal classification (ORD), and a linear-chain conditional random field (CRF) for making a conditioned decision on the whole sequence.

Softmax Layer. For the SOFTMAX-layer, the model predicts a normalized distribution over all possible labels (L) for every word conditioned on the hidden vector (h_t).

Relaxed Softmax Layer. In contrast, the ORD-layer uses a standard sigmoid projection for every output label candidate, without subjecting it to normalization. The intuition is that rather than learning to predict one label per word, the model predicts multiple labels. For a word with label $l \in L$, all other labels ordinally less than l are also predicted. Both the softmax and the relaxed-softmax models are trained to minimize the categorical cross-entropy, which is equivalent to minimizing the negative log-probability of the correct labels. However, they differ in how they make the final prediction: Unlike the SOFTMAX layer which considers the most probable label for prediction, the ORD-layer uses a special "scanning" strategy (Cheng et al., 2008) – where for each word, the candidate labels are scanned from low to high (ordinal rank), until the score from a label is smaller than a threshold (usually 0.5) or no labels remain. The last scanned label with score greater than the threshold is selected as the output.

CRF Layer. The CRF-layer explores the possible dependence between the subsequent importance label of words. With this architecture, the network looks for the most optimal path through all possible label sequences to make the prediction. The model is then optimized by maximizing the score of the correct sequence of labels, while minimizing the possibility of all other possible sequences. Considering each of these different projection layers, we investigate different models for the word importance prediction task. Section 4 describes our architecture for acoustic-prosodic feature representation at the word level, and Sections 5 and 6 describe our experimental setup and subsequent evaluations.

4 Acoustic-Prosodic Feature Representation

Similar to familiar feature-vector representations of words in a text e.g., word2vec (Mikolov et al., 2013) or GloVe (Pennington et al., 2014), various researchers have investigated vector representations of words based on speech. In addition to capturing acoustic-phonetic properties of speech (He et al., 2017; Chung et al., 2016), some recent work on acoustic embeddings has investigated encoding semantic properties of a word directly from speech (Chung and Glass, 2018). In a similar way, our work investigates a speech-based feature representation strategy that considers prosodic features of speech at a sub-word level, to learn a word-level representation for the task of importance prediction in spoken dialogue.

4.1 Sub-word Feature Extraction

We examined four categories of features that have been previously considered in computational models of prosody, including: pitch-related features (10), energy features (11), voicing features (3) and spoken-lexical features (6):

• **Pitch (FREQ) and Energy (ENG) Features:** Pitch and energy features have been found effective for modeling intonation and detecting emphasized regions of speech (Brenier et al., 2005). From the pitch and energy contours of the speech, we extracted: minimum, time of minimum, maximum, time of maximum, mean, median, range, slope, standard deviation and skewness. We also extracted RMS energy from a mid-range frequency band (500-2000 Hz), which has been shown to be useful for detecting prominence of syllables in speech (Tamburini, 2003).

• **Spoken-lexical Features (LEX):** We examined spoken-lexical features, including word-level spoken language features such as duration of the spoken word, the position of the word in the utterance, and duration of silence before the word. We also estimated the number of syllables spoken in a word, using the methodology of De Jong and Wempe (2009). Further, we considered the per-word average syllable duration and the per-word articulation rate of the speaker (number of syllables per second).

• **Voicing Features (VOC):** As a measure of voice quality, we investigated spectral-tilt, which is represented as (H1 - H2), i.e. the difference between the amplitudes of the first harmonic (H1) and the second harmonic (H2) in the Fourier Spectrum. The spectral-tilt measure has been shown to be effective in characterizing glottal constriction (Keating and Esposito, 2006), which is important in distinguishing voicing characteristics, e.g. whisper (Ito et al., 2002). We also exmined other voicing measures, e.g. Harmonics-to-Noise Ratio and Voiced Unvoiced Ratio.

In total, we extracted 30 features using Praat (Boersma, 2006), as listed above. Further, we included speaker-normalized (ZNORM) version of the features. Thereby, we had a total of 60 speech-based features extracted from sub-word units.

4.2 Sub-word to Word-level Representation

The acoustic features listed above were extracted from a 50-ms sliding window over each word region with a 10-ms overlap. In our model, each word was represented as a sequence of these sub-word features with varying lengths, as shown in Figure 2. To get a feature representation for a word, we utilized a bi-directional Recurrent Neural Network (RNN) layer on top of the sub-word features. The spoken-lexical features were then concatenated to this word-level feature representation to get our final feature vectors. For this task, we utilized Gated Recurrent Units (GRUs) (Cho et al., 2014) as our RNN cell, rather than LSTM units, due to better performance observed during our initial analysis.

5 Experimental Setup

We utilized a portion of the Switchboard corpus (Godfrey et al., 1992) that had been manually annotated with word importance scores, as a part of the Word Importance Annotation project (Kafle and Huenerfauth, 2018). That annotation covers 25,048 utterances spoken by 44 different English speakers, containing word-level timestamp information along with a numeric score (in the range of [0, 1]) assigned to each word from the speakers. These numeric importance scores have three natural ordinal ranges [0 - 0.3), [0.3, 0.6), [0.6, 1] that the annotators had used during the annotation to indicate the importance of a word in understanding an utterance. The ordinal range represents low importance (LI), medium importance (MI) and high importance (HI) of words, respectively.

Our models were trained and evaluated using this data, treating the problem as a ordinal classification problem with the labels ordered as (LI $<$ MI $<$ HI). We created a 80%, 10% and 10% split of our data for training, validation, and testing. The prediction performance of our model was primarily evaluated using the Root Mean Square (RMS) measure, to account for the ordinal nature of labels. Additionally, our evaluation includes F-score and accuracy results to measure classification performance. As our baseline, we used various text-based importance prediction models trained and evaluated on the same data split, as described in Section 6.3.

For training, we explored various architectural parameters to find the best-working setup for our models: Our input layer of GRU-cells, used as word-based speech representation, had a dimension of 64. The LSTM units, used for generating contextualized representation of a spoken word, had a dimension of 128. We used the Adam optimizer with an initialized learning rate of 0.001 for training. Each training batch had a maximum of 20 dialogue-turn utterances, and the model was trained until no improvement was observed in 7 consecutive iterations.

6 Experiments

Tables 1, 2 and 3 summarize the performance of our models on the word importance prediction task. The performance scores reported in the tables are the average performance across 5 different trials, to account for possible bias due to random initialization of the model.

6.1 Comparison of the Projection Layers

We compared the efficacy of the learning architecture's three projection layers (Section 3.1) by training them separately and comparing their performance on the test corpus. Table 1 summarizes the results of this evaluation.

Results and Analysis: The LSTM-SOFTMAX-based and LSTM-CRF-based projection layers had nearly identical performance; however, in comparison, the LSTM-ORD model had better performance with significantly lower RMS score than the other two models. This suggests the utility of the ordinal constraint present in the ORD-based model for word importance classification.

Model	ACC	F1	RMS
LSTM-CRF	64.22	56.31	75.21
LSTM-SOFTMAX	**65.66**	57.34	74.08
LSTM-ORD	63.72	**57.58**	**68.21**

Table 1: Performance of our speech-based models on the test data under different projection layers. Best performing scores highlighted in **bold**.

6.2 Ablation Study on Speech Features

To compare the effect of different categories of speech features on the performance of our model, we evaluated variations of the model by removing one feature group at a time from the model during training. Table 2 summarizes the results of the experiment.

Model	ACC	F1	RMS
speech-based	63.72	57.58	68.21
– ENG	62.24†	55.67†	71.14
– FREQ	63.25	57.30	69.0
– VOC	62.90	56.84	70.5
– LEX	63.37	57.34	71.49†
– ZNORM	62.04*	53.86*	72.0*

Table 2: Speech feature ablation study. The minus sign indicates the feature group removed from the model during training. Markers ($\star$ and $\dagger$) indicate the biggest and the second-biggest change in model performance for each metric, respectively.

Results and Analysis: Omitting speaker-based normalization (ZNORM) features and omitting spoken-lexical features (LEX) resulted in the greatest increase in the overall RMS error (+5.5% and +4.8% relative increase in RMS respectively) – suggesting the discriminative importance of these features for word importance prediction. Further, our results indicated the importance of energy-based (ENG) features, which resulted in a substantial drop (-2.4% relative decrease) in accuracy of the model.

6.3 Comparison with the Text-based Models

In this analysis, we compare our best-performing speech-based model with a state-of-the-art word-prediction model based on text features; this prior text-based model did not utilize any acoustic or prosodic information about the speech signal. The baseline text-based word importance prediction model used in our analysis is described in Kafle and Huenerfauth (2018), and it uses pre-trained word embeddings and bi-direction LSTM units, with a CRF layer on top, to make a prediction for each word.

As discussed in Section 1, human transcriptions are difficult to obtain in some applications, e.g. real-time conversational settings. Realistically, text-based models need to rely on ASR systems for transcription, which will contain some errors. Thus, we compare our speech-based model and this prior text-based model on two different types of transcripts: manually generated or ASR generated. We processed the original speech recording for each segment of the corpus with an ASR system to produce an automatic transcription. To simulate different word error rate (WER) levels in the transcript, we also artificially injected the original speech recording with white-noise and then processed it again with our ASR system. Specifically, we utilized Google Cloud Speech[2] ASR with WER$\approx$ 25% on our test data (without the addition of noise) and WER$\approx$ 30% after noise was inserted. Given our interest in generating automatic captions for DHH users in a live meeting on a turn-by-turn basis (Section 1), we provided the ASR system with the recording for each dialogue-turn individually, which may partially explain these somewhat high WER scores.

The automatically generated transcripts were then aligned with the reference transcript to compare the importance scores. Insertion errors automatically received a label of low importance (LI). The WER for each ASR system was computed by performing a word-to-word comparison, without any pre-processing (e.g., removal of filler words).

Model	ACC	F1	RMS
speech-based	63.72	57.58	68.21
text-based	77.81	73.6	54.0
+ WER: **0.25**	72.30	69.04	65.15
+ WER: **0.30**	71.84	67.71	68.55

Table 3: Comparison of our speech-based model with a prior text-based model, under different word error rate conditions.

Result and Analysis: Given the significant lexical information available for the text-based model, it would be natural to expect that it would achieve higher scores than would a model based only on acoustic-prosodic features. As expected, Table 3 reveals that when operating on perfect human-generated transcripts (with zero recognition errors), the text-based model outperformed our speech-based model. However, when operating on ASR transcripts (including recognition errors), the speech-based models were competitive in performance with the text-based models. In particular, prior work has found that WER of $\approx$ 30% is typical for modern ASR in many real-world settings or without good-quality microphones (Lasecki et al., 2012; Barker et al., 2017). When operating on such ASR output, the RMS error of the speech-based model and the text-based model were comparable.

7 Conclusion

Motivated by recent work on evaluating the accuracy of automatic speech recognition systems for real-time captioning for Deaf and Hard of Hearing (DHH) users (Kafle and Huenerfauth, 2018), we investigated how to predict the importance of a word to the overall meaning of a spoken conversation turn. In contrast to prior work, which had depended on text-based features, we have proposed a neural architecture for modeling prosodic cues in spoken messages, for predicting word importance. Our text-independent speech model had an F-score of 56 in a 3-class word importance classification task. Although a text-based model utilizing pre-trained word representation had better performance, acquisition of accurate speech conversation text-transcripts is impractical for some applications. When utilizing popular ASR systems to automatically generate speech transcripts as input for text-based models, we found that model performance decreased significantly. Given this potential we observed for acoustic-prosodic features to predict word importance continued work involves combining both text- and speech-based features for the task of word importance prediction.

8 Acknowledgements

This material was based on work supported by the Department of Health and Human Services under Award No. 90DPCP0002-01-00, by a Google Faculty Research Award, and by the National Technical Institute of the Deaf (NTID).

[2] `https://cloud.google.com/Speech_API`

References

Jon P. Barker, Ricard Marxer, Emmanuel Vincent, and Shinji Watanabe. 2017. The chime challenges: Robust speech recognition in everyday environments. In Shinji Watanabe, Marc Delcroix, Florian Metze, and John R. Hershey, editors, *New Era for Robust Speech Recognition, Exploiting Deep Learning.*, pages 327–344. Springer.

Mary E Beckman and Jennifer J Venditti. 2000. Tagging prosody and discourse structure in elicited spontaneous speech.

Larwan Berke, Sushant Kafle, and Matt Huenerfauth. 2018. Methods for evaluation of imperfect captioning tools by deaf or hard-of-hearing users at different reading literacy levels. In *Proceedings of the 2018 CHI Conference on Human Factors in Computing Systems*, CHI '18, pages 91:1–91:12, New York, NY, USA. ACM.

Paul Boersma. 2006. Praat: doing phonetics by computer. *http://www. praat. org/.*

Jason M. Brenier, Daniel M. Cer, and Daniel Jurafsky. 2005. The detection of emphatic words using acoustic and lexical features. In *INTERSPEECH 2005 - Eurospeech, 9th European Conference on Speech Communication and Technology, Lisbon, Portugal, September 4-8, 2005*, pages 3297–3300. ISCA.

Jianlin Cheng, Zheng Wang, and Gianluca Pollastri. 2008. A neural network approach to ordinal regression. In *Proc. of IJCNN 2008, Hong Kong, China, June 1-6, 2008*, pages 1279–1284. IEEE.

Kyunghyun Cho, Bart van Merrienboer, Dzmitry Bahdanau, and Yoshua Bengio. 2014. On the properties of neural machine translation: Encoder-decoder approaches. In *Proc. of SSST@EMNLP 2014, Eighth Workshop on Syntax, Semantics and Structure in Statistical Translation, Doha, Qatar, 25 October 2014*, pages 103–111. Association for Computational Linguistics.

Yu-An Chung and James R. Glass. 2018. Speech2vec: A sequence-to-sequence framework for learning word embeddings from speech. In *Interspeech 2018, 19th Annual Conference of the International Speech Communication Association, Hyderabad, India, 2-6 September 2018.*, pages 811–815. ISCA.

Yu-An Chung, Chao-Chung Wu, Chia-Hao Shen, Hung-yi Lee, and Lin-Shan Lee. 2016. Audio word2vec: Unsupervised learning of audio segment representations using sequence-to-sequence autoencoder. In *Interspeech 2016, 17th Annual Conference of the International Speech Communication Association, San Francisco, CA, USA, September 8-12, 2016*, pages 765–769. ISCA.

Nivja H De Jong and Ton Wempe. 2009. Praat script to detect syllable nuclei and measure speech rate automatically. *Behavior research methods*, 41(2):385–390.

Lyn Frazier, Katy Carlson, and Charles Clifton. 2006. Prosodic phrasing is central to language comprehension. *Trends in cognitive sciences*, 10(6):244–249.

John J Godfrey, Edward C Holliman, and Jane McDaniel. 1992. Switchboard: Telephone speech corpus for research and development. In *Acoustics, Speech, and Signal Processing, 1992. ICASSP-92., 1992 IEEE International Conference on*, volume 1, pages 517–520. IEEE.

Yaakov HaCohen-Kerner, Zuriel Gross, and Asaf Masa. 2005. Automatic extraction and learning of keyphrases from scientific articles. In *Proc. of CICLing 2005, Mexico City, Mexico, February 13-19, 2005*, volume 3406, pages 657–669. Springer.

Wanjia He, Weiran Wang, and Karen Livescu. 2017. Multi-view recurrent neural acoustic word embeddings. In *Proc. of ICLR 2017, Toulon, France, April 24-26, 2017*. OpenReview.net.

Kai Hong and Ani Nenkova. 2014. Improving the estimation of word importance for news multi-document summarization. In *Proc. of EACL 2014, April 26-30, 2014, Gothenburg, Sweden*, pages 712–721. The Association for Computer Linguistics.

Zhiheng Huang, Wei Xu, and Kai Yu. 2015. Bidirectional LSTM-CRF models for sequence tagging. *CoRR*, abs/1508.01991.

Anette Hulth. 2003. Improved automatic keyword extraction given more linguistic knowledge. In *Proc. of EMNLP 2003, Sapporo, Japan, July 11-12, 2003.*

Taisuke Ito, Kazuya Takeda, and Fumitada Itakura. 2002. Acoustic analysis and recognition of whispered speech. In *Proc. of ICASSP 2002, May 13-17 2002, Orlando, Florida, USA*, pages 389–392. IEEE.

Sushant Kafle and Matt Huenerfauth. 2017. Evaluating the usability of automatically generated captions for people who are deaf or hard of hearing. In *Proceedings of the 19th International ACM SIGACCESS Conference on Computers and Accessibility, ASSETS 2017, Baltimore, MD, USA, October 29 - November 01, 2017*, pages 165–174. ACM.

Sushant Kafle and Matt Huenerfauth. 2018. A corpus for modeling word importance in spoken dialogue transcripts. In *Proceedings of the Eleventh International Conference on Language Resources and Evaluation, LREC 2018, Miyazaki, Japan, May 7-12, 2018.* European Language Resources Association (ELRA).

Patricia A Keating and Christina Esposito. 2006. Linguistic voice quality. *UCLA Working Papers in Phonetics*, 105(6).

Guillaume Lample, Miguel Ballesteros, Sandeep Subramanian, Kazuya Kawakami, and Chris Dyer. 2016. Neural architectures for named entity recognition. In *Proc. of NAACL HLT 2016, San Diego California,*

USA, June 12-17, 2016, pages 260–270. The Association for Computational Linguistics.

Walter S. Lasecki, Christopher D. Miller, Adam Sadilek, Andrew Abumoussa, Donato Borrello, Raja S. Kushalnagar, and Jeffrey P. Bigham. 2012. Real-time captioning by groups of non-experts. In *The 25th Annual ACM Symposium on User Interface Software and Technology, UIST '12, Cambridge, MA, USA, October 7-10, 2012*, pages 23–34. ACM.

Bing Liu, Xiaoli Li, Wee Sun Lee, and Philip S. Yu. 2004. Text classification by labeling words. In *Proc. of AAAI, July 25-29, 2004, San Jose, California, USA*, pages 425–430. AAAI Press / The MIT Press.

Fei Liu, Feifan Liu, and Yang Liu. 2011. A supervised framework for keyword extraction from meeting transcripts. *IEEE Trans. Audio, Speech & Language Processing*, 19(3):538–548.

Yutaka Matsuo and Mitsuru Ishizuka. 2004. Keyword extraction from a single document using word co-occurrence statistical information. *International Journal on Artificial Intelligence Tools*, 13(1):157–169.

Iain A. McCowan, Darren Moore, John Dines, Daniel Gatica-Perez, Mike Flynn, Pierre Wellner, and Hervé Bourlard. 2004. On the use of information retrieval measures for speech recognition evaluation. Idiap-RR Idiap-RR-73-2004, IDIAP, Martigny, Switzerland.

Kathleen R. McKeown, Julia Hirschberg, Michel Galley, and Sameer Maskey. 2005. From text to speech summarization. In *2005 IEEE International Conference on Acoustics, Speech, and Signal Processing, ICASSP '05, Philadelphia, Pennsylvania, USA, March 18-23, 2005*, pages 997–1000. IEEE.

Tomas Mikolov, Ilya Sutskever, Kai Chen, Gregory S. Corrado, and Jeffrey Dean. 2013. Distributed representations of words and phrases and their compositionality. In *Advances in Neural Information Processing Systems 26: 27th Annual Conference on Neural Information Processing Systems 2013. Proceedings of a meeting held December 5-8, 2013, Lake Tahoe, Nevada, United States.*, pages 3111–3119.

Taniya Mishra, Vivek Kumar Rangarajan Sridhar, and Alistair Conkie. 2012. Word prominence detection using robust yet simple prosodic features. In *INTERSPEECH 2012, 13th Annual Conference of the International Speech Communication Association, Portland, Oregon, USA, September 9-13, 2012*, pages 1864–1867. ISCA.

Andrew Cameron Morris, Viktoria Maier, and Phil D. Green. 2004. From WER and RIL to MER and WIL: improved evaluation measures for connected speech recognition. In *INTERSPEECH 2004 - ICSLP, 8th International Conference on Spoken Language Processing, Jeju Island, Korea, October 4-8, 2004*.

Gabriel Murray, Steve Renals, and Jean Carletta. 2005. Extractive summarization of meeting recordings. In *INTERSPEECH 2005 - Eurospeech, 9th European Conference on Speech Communication and Technology, Lisbon, Portugal, September 4-8, 2005*, pages 593–596. ISCA.

Jeffrey Pennington, Richard Socher, and Christopher D. Manning. 2014. Glove: Global vectors for word representation. In *Proc. of EMNLP 2014, October 25-29, 2014, Doha, Qatar.*, pages 1532–1543. ACL.

Patti Price, Mari Ostendorf, Stefanie Shattuck-Hufnagel, and Cynthia Fong. 1991. The use of prosody in syntactic disambiguation. In *Speech and Natural Language, Proceedings of a Workshop held at Pacific Grove, California, USA, February 19-22. 1991*. Morgan Kaufmann.

JI Sheeba and K Vivekanandan. 2012. Improved keyword and keyphrase extraction from meeting transcripts. *International Journal of Computer Applications*, 52(13).

Imran A. Sheikh, Irina Illina, Dominique Fohr, and Georges Linarès. 2016. Learning word importance with the neural bag-of-words model. In *Proc. of Rep4NLP@ACL 2016, Berlin, Germany, August 11, 2016*, pages 222–229. Association for Computational Linguistics.

Fabio Tamburini. 2003. Prosodic prominence detection in speech. In *Seventh International Symposium on Signal Processing and Its Applications, ISSPA 2003, July 1-4, 2003, Paris, France, Proceedings, Volume 1*, pages 385–388. IEEE.

Trang Tran, Shubham Toshniwal, Mohit Bansal, Kevin Gimpel, Karen Livescu, and Mari Ostendorf. 2017. Joint modeling of text and acoustic-prosodic cues for neural parsing. *CoRR*, abs/1704.07287.

Dagen Wang and Shrikanth Narayanan. 2007. An acoustic measure for word prominence in spontaneous speech. *IEEE Trans. Audio, Speech & Language Processing*, 15(2):690–701.

Shasha Xie, Dilek Hakkani-Tür, Benoît Favre, and Yang Liu. 2009. Integrating prosodic features in extractive meeting summarization. In *2009 IEEE Workshop on Automatic Speech Recognition & Understanding, ASRU 2009, Merano/Meran, Italy, December 13-17, 2009*, pages 387–391. IEEE.

Wen-tau Yih, Joshua Goodman, Lucy Vanderwende, and Hisami Suzuki. 2007. Multi-document summarization by maximizing informative content-words. In *Proc. of IJCAI 2007, Hyderabad, India, January 6-12, 2007*, pages 1776–1782.

Permanent Magnetic Articulograph (PMA) vs Electromagnetic Articulograph (EMA) in Articulation-to-Speech Synthesis for Silent Speech Interface

Beiming Cao[1], Nordine Sebkhi[3], Ted Mau[4], Omer T. Inan[3],Jun Wang[1,2]
[1]Speech Disorders & Technology Lab, Department of Bioengineering
[2]Callier Center for Communication Disorders
University of Texas at Dallas, Richardson, TX, USA
[3] Inan Research Lab, School of Electrical and Computer Engineering
Georgia Institute of Technology, Atlanta, GA, USA
[4] Department of Otolaryngology - Head and Neck Surgery
University of Texas Southwestern Medical Center, Dallas, TX, USA

Abstract

Silent speech interfaces (SSIs) are devices that enable speech communication when audible speech is unavailable. Articulation-to-speech (ATS) synthesis is a software design in SSI that directly converts articulatory movement information into audible speech signals. Permanent magnetic articulograph (PMA) is a wireless articulator motion tracking technology that is similar to commercial, wired Electromagnetic Articulograph (EMA). PMA has shown great potential for practical SSI applications, because it is wireless. The ATS performance of PMA, however, is unknown when comparing with current EMA. In this study, we compared the performance of ATS using a PMA we recently developed and a commercially available EMA (NDI Wave system). Datasets with same stimuli and size that were collected from tongue tip were used in the comparison. The experimental results indicated the performance of PMA was close to, although not as equally good as that of EMA. Furthermore, in PMA, converting the raw magnetic signals to positional signals did not significantly affect the performance of ATS, which support the future direction in PMA-based ATS can be focused on the use of positional signals to maximize the benefit of spatial analysis.

1 Introduction

People who had a laryngectomy have their larynx surgically removed in the treatment of a condition such as laryngeal cancer (Bailey et al., 2006). The removal of the larynx, as a treatment of cancer, prevents laryngectomees from producing speech sounds and inhibit their ability to communicate. Current approaches for improving their ability to communicate include (intra- or extra-oral) artificial larynx (Baraff, 1994), tracheoesophageal puncture (TEP) (Robbins et al., 1984), and esophageal speech (Hyman, 1955). All of these approaches generate abnormal speech like hoarse voicing by tracheoesophageal speech or robotic voicing by artificial larynx (Mau, 2010; Mau et al., 2012). These patients may feel depressed because of their health status and anxiety during social interactions, as they think that other people perceive them as abnormal, or they directly experience symbolic violence (Mertl et al., 2018). As a result, the development of communication aids that can produce normal-sounding speech is essential to improving the quality of life for patients in this population.

Silent speech interfaces (SSI) are devices which convert non-audio biological signals, such as movement of articulators, to audible speech (Denby et al., 2010). Unlike existing methods, SSIs are able to produce natural sounding synthesized speech and even have the potential to recover the patients' own voices. There are currently two types of software designs in SSI. One is a "recognition-and-synthesis" approach, which is to convert articulatory movement to text, and then drive speech output using a text-to-speech synthesizer (Kim et al., 2017). The other design is direct articulation-to-speech (ATS) synthesis, which is more promising for SSI application, because ATS can be real-time. Currently, the prominent methods for capturing articulatory motion data include: electromagnetic articulograph (EMA) (Schönle et al., 1987; Cao et al., 2018; Bocquelet et al., 2016), permanent magnet articulograph (PMA) (Gonzalez et al., 2014; Kim et al., 2018), ultrasound image (Csapó et al., 2017), surface electromyography (sEMG) (Diener et al., 2018), non-audible murmur (NAM) (Nakajima et al., 2003). All of these technologies have

Proceedings of the Eighth Workshop on Speech and Language Processing for Assistive Technologies, pages 17–23
Minneapolis, Minnesota, USA ©2019 Association for Computational Linguistics

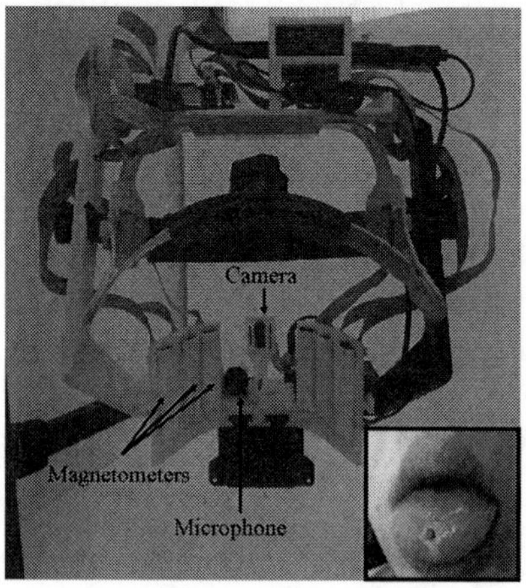

Figure 1: Our recently developed, head-set PMA device, where a small magnet is attached on the tongue tip.

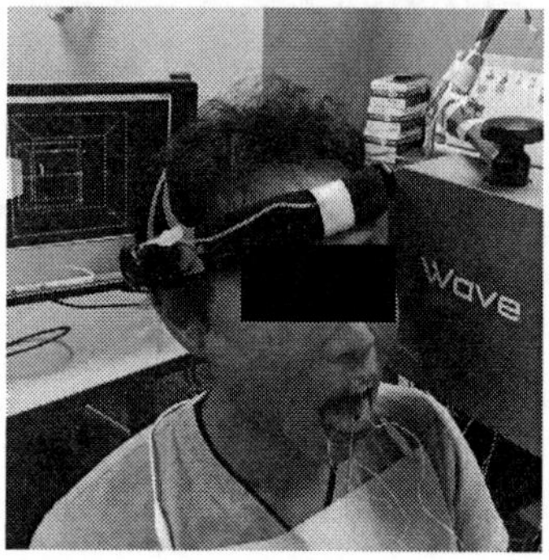

Figure 2: Wave System (EMA), where multiple sensors are attached on the tongue and lips. Only the tongue tip sensor data was used in the comparison with PMA.

their own advantages and disadvantages. PMA has recently shown its potential for SSI because it is wireless and suitable for future practical applications.

Unlike EMA that uses wired sensors attached on the articulators with a magnetic field generator outside, PMA attaches (wireless) permanent magnets to articulators and adopts magnetometers to capture the changes in the magnetic field generated by the motion of the magnets. These magnetic readings are then fed into a localization algorithm that estimates the 3D position of the magnet in the oral cavity (Sebkhi et al., 2017). Both EMA and PMA have been used in prior research on ATS (Cao et al., 2018; Gonzalez et al., 2017a; Cheah et al., 2018) with varying results. Although EMA has been shown to yield more precise measurements (Yunusova et al., 2009; Berry, 2011) compared to PMA (Sebkhi et al., 2017), EMA devices are normally cumbersome as they require wired sensors be attached to articulators. Additionally, EMA devices are normally expensive. In contrast, PMA devices are mostly very light and portable, relying on wireless tracking by using permanent magnets as the tracers, also affordable compared to EMA. Due to the wireless, portability and low-cost advantages of PMA, it offers an appealing alternative to EMA if it is able to achieve similar levels of performance as EMA in ATS systems. To our knowledge, however, no prior studies have directly compared the performance of these two technologies for SSI applications.

In this study, we compared the ATS performance of our recently developed PMA-based wireless tongue tracking system and a commercial EMA (NDI Wave system). We first examined whether it is more effective to use raw magnetic field signals than to use the converted magnet positional data (x, y, z coordinates) of PMA in ATS. Second, we compared the performance of EMA and PMA using tongue tip data only. A deep neural network (DNN)-based ATS model was used to evaluate the ATS performance for both EMA and PMA data. In this study, a dataset was collected from two groups of subjects who spoke the same stimuli using PMA or EMA, respectively. Tongue tip is the common flesh point in the PMA and EMA datasets, which were used for analysis in this study.

2 Dataset

2.1 PMA Data Collection

Ten subjects (6 males and 4 females, average age: 24.1 years $\pm$ 4.84) participated in the PMA data collection session in which they repeated a list of 132 phrases twice in their habitual speaking rate. The first repetition is normal voiced speech, and the second repetition is unvoiced speech. In this study, only the voiced speech data was used. The phrases in the list were phrases that are frequently spoken by users of augmentative and alternative communication (AAC) devices (Glennen and DeCoste, 1997). The PMA data was collected at the Georgia Institute of Technology.

The PMA data used in this study was collected with our newly developed wearable, headset system, which is based on the same magnetic technology in the prior benchtop version multimodal speech capture system (MSCS) (Sebkhi et al.,

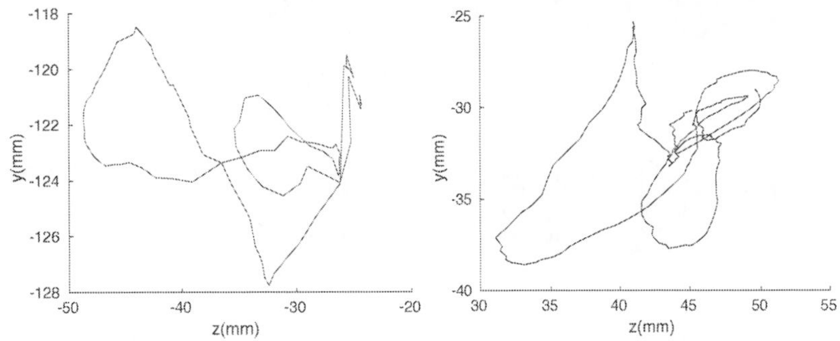

(a) EMA (b) PMA

Figure 3: Lateral view samples of tongue tip trajectory captured by PMA and EMA when saying: "That is perfect!" (By two different subjects).

2017). Figure 1 shows the wearable, wireless tongue tracking system, which uses PMA and a camera for tongue and lip motion caption, respectively. A microphone was used for audio recording. This PMA system has an embedded array of magnetometers that measure the change of magnetic field generated by a magnetic tracer attached close to the tongue tip.

During a data collection session, a disk-shaped magnetic tracer (diameter = 3mm, thickness = 1.5mm, D21BN52, K&J Magnetics) was attached to about 1cm from tongue tip. An array of 24 external 3-axial magnetometers (LSM303D, STMicroelectronics) are divided into six modules, each with 4 magnetometers, which are positioned near the mouth, so there are two groups of 12 sensors that are near the right cheek and left cheek. These sensors were used for capturing the magnetic field fluctuations generated by the tracer, which are fed into a localization algorithm that estimates the 3D position of the magnet every 10 ms (100 Hz). The spatial tracking accuracy of the PMA varies from 0.44 to 2.94 mm depending upon the position and orientation of the tracer (Sebkhi et al., 2017). The audio data recording was sampled at 96000 Hz.

Previous studies (Gonzalez et al., 2017a; Cheah et al., 2018) show that the combination of multiple tracers on the tongue had better performance than single tracer (i.e., tongue tip). However, a smaller number of magnetic tracers on the tongue is critical for its practical use in daily life (Kim et al., 2018). Future users of this technology likely prefer to have only one permanent or semi-permanent attached magnetic tracer on their tongue. Even for lab experiment, attaching multiple tracers on the tongue takes longer time and relative logistic difficulty to operate. In addition, with only one tracer on the tongue tip, the risk of accidentally biting it is very small (Laumann et al., 2015).

To provide the best tracking performance with one single tracer, the system relies on 24 magnetometers positioned outside the mount to accurately track the tongue motion (Kim et al., 2018). The six magnetometer modules are connected via serial peripheral interface (SPI) to a sensor controller module (Kim et al., 2018) that also includes a USB interface to communicate with the PC. More technical details about the tracking technology can be found in (Sebkhi et al., 2017). In this study, although wearable, the headset was anchored to a support in order to provide the best positional accuracy (to avoid possible head motion during recording).

2.2 EMA Data Collection

Another group of 10 gender- and age-matched subjects (6 males and 4 females, average age: 24.3 years $\pm$ 3.50) participated in the EMA data collection session. These individuals read the same list of 132 phrases used in the PMA data collection session. The EMA dataset was collected at the University of Texas at Dallas.

Wave system (Northern Digital Inc., Waterloo, Canada) was used for EMA data collection (Figure 2). Four small wired sensors were attached to the tongue tip (0.5 to 1cm from tongue apex), tongue back (20-30mm back from TT), upper lip and lower lip using dental glue or tape. Additionally, a fifth (head) sensor was attached to the middle of forehead for head correction. Finally, 3D EMA data was sampled at 100 Hz which is same to PMA data. The spatial precision of motion tracking is

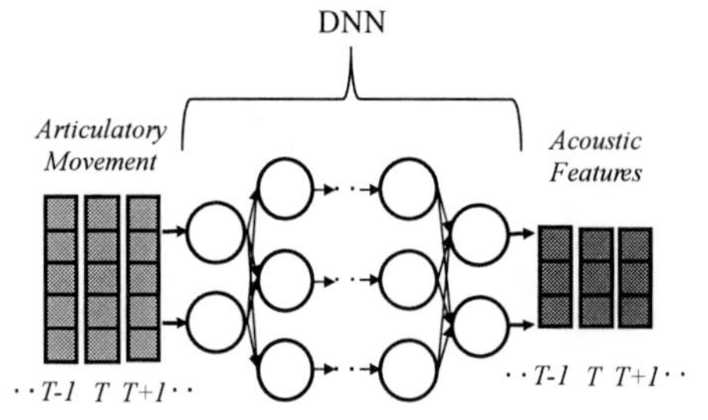

Figure 4: ATS using DNN.

about 0.5 mm (Berry, 2011), Figure 3(a) gives an example of two-dimensional (2D) EMA tongue tip movement trajectory (lateral view) when saying: "That is perfect!". The sampling rate of audio data was 22050 Hz. NDI Wave system does not provide the raw magnetic signals.

To ensure an analogous comparison with the PMA device, only the tongue tip data collected using EMA was used in this study.

2.3 Data Preprocessing

To provide EMA and PMA consistent acoustic features, the sampling rates of audio data in EMA and PMA were resampled to same level. The audio data in PMA dataset was downsampled to 48000 Hz from 96000 Hz, and the audio data in EMA dataset was upsampled to 48000 Hz from 22050 Hz. After that, spectral envelope was extracted with Cheaptrick algorithm (Morise, 2015) and then converted to 60-dimensional mel-cepstral coefficients (MCCs) as the output acoustic features of ATS model. The MCCs were extracted at a rate of 200 frames per second, therefore, the PMA and EMA data were upsampled to 200 Hz to match the acoustic features.

Our PMA device captures the motion of tongue tip with the 72-channel raw magnet signals (3 axes 24 magnetometers). In addition to raw magnet signals, the 3D cartesian positions of the magnet tracer were obtained by localizing the raw magnet signals with nonlinear optimization method (Sebkhi et al., 2017). Figure 3(b) gives an example of a 2D trajectory (lateral view) of magnet tracer when saying "That is perfect!" obtained by localizing raw magnet signals. Both raw magnet signals and 3D-position signals were used in this study.

3 Method

3.1 Articulation-to-Speech Synthesis (ATS) Using Deep Neural Network (DNN)

The ATS model in this study uses a DNN to map articulatory signals (PMA or EMA) to acoustic features (MCCs) (Figure 4).The first and second order derivatives of both input articulatory and the output acoustic data frames were computed and concatenated to the original frames for context information.

The DNN has 6 hidden layers, each layer has 512 nodes with rectified linear unit (ReLU) activation function. During the DNN training, Adam optimizer (Kingma and Ba, 2014) was used, the maximum number of training epochs is 50, learning rate for PMA data is 0.008 and 0.005 for EMA data. The performances of ATS system is assessed using EMA positional data, PMA raw data, PMA positional data, and the combination of PMA raw and positional data. Therefore, the input dimensions of ATS in this study are: 9 (3-dim. PMA or EMA positional + Δ + $\Delta\Delta$), 216 (72-dim. PMA raw magnet signals + Δ + $\Delta\Delta$), and 225 (concatenation of 9-dim. and 216-dim.). The output dimension is 180 (60-dim. MCCs + Δ + $\Delta\Delta$). The DNN model in this study was implemented with Tensorflow machine learning library (Abadi et al., 2016).

3.2 Experimental Setup

As mentioned previously, we first compared the ATS performance using raw PMA signals, converted positional data, or both. This experiment will help to understand the which type of PMA data leads to the best performance. NDI Wave is a commercial system, which does not provide any magnetic signals that have not been localized, thus this experiment was conducted for our PMA system only. Second, we compared the best performance in PMA with the performance in EMA. The results will reveal which technology (PMA or EMA) performs better.

Speaker-dependent setup was used in both experiments, as speaker-independent ATS is considered challenging at this moment, due to the physiological difference among different speakers. The ATS performances on each subject were averaged as the final performance. For the 132 phrases in both PMA and EMA data, 110 phrases were used for training, 10 for validating, and 12 for testing.

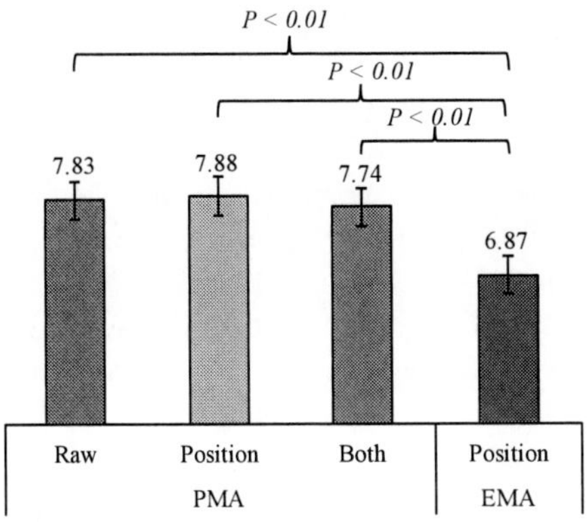

Figure 5: Average MCD of 10 PMA Subjects and 10 EMA Subjects. Statistical significances between the results using EMA and all types of PMA data on ATS model are computed with ANOVA tests.

The ATS results were measured with mel-cepstral distortion (MCD). MCD is calculated by equation (1), where C and C^{gen} denote the original and generated mel-cepstral coefficients (MCCs), respectively, m is the frame step (or time), d denotes dth dimension in frame m. D is the dimension of MCCs, which is 60 in this study.

$$MCD = \frac{10}{ln10} \sum_{m=1}^{T} \sqrt{2 \sum_{d=1}^{D} (C_{m,d} - C_{m,d}^{gen})^2} \quad (1)$$

As mentioned, lip movement information has not been used in this study, since PMA and EMA devices use different approaches for lip motion caption. PMA uses a computer vision algorithm to recognize the shape of the lips from images captured by an embedded camera, whereas EMA relies on tracking the motion of attached sensors to the vermilion borders of the lips to estimate lips gesture. In additon, due to the relatively small data size, the synthesized audio samples did not have sufficiently high speech intelligibility for listening test. Therefore, the subjective/listening testing was not conducted in this study.

4 Results and Discussion

4.1 Magnetic signals vs positional data in PMA

Experimental results are presented in Figure 5, where three-way ANOVA tests were used in the statistical analysis. First, for PMA, that performance using raw magnet data was not significantly different to the performance using positional data only ($p < 0.85$), and was also not significantly different with that using combined raw magnetic field signals and positional data ($p < 0.76$). There was also no significance between the ATS performance using positional data only and that using combined raw magnetic field signals and positional data ($p < 0.60$).

These findings suggest, for PMA, we could use either raw magnetic field signals or converted positional data for a similar level of performance. Combining these two signals together may not improve the performance. This finding is inconsistent with our prior study in silent speech recognition (SSR) using PMA data, where using magnetic signals outperformed than that using converted positional data (Kim et al., 2018). Further studies are needed to reveal why magnetic signals outperformed positional data in SSR, but their performance in ATS was not significantly different.

The finding that positional data can have similar performance with that using magnetic data is encouraging for our future development of ATS using PMA. Although mapping the raw magnetic signals directly to acoustic features is more straightforward, transforming these signals to positional signals allows the use of articulation data processing methods, such as Procrustes matching (Gower, 1975; Kim et al., 2017), that cannot be easily applied to the raw data. In addition, a PMA positional data-based ATS can be decoupled from a device configuration, it will be easier to change the number of sensors, their positions, their model, and their settings. Finally, a PMA positional data-based ATS has a potential of using EMA data for training, since they both track the 3D motion of articulators.

4.2 PMA vs EMA

Second, when comparing the ATS performance using PMA data and EMA data, the results obtained using PMA is not as equally good as that obtained in EMA. The performance in EMA significantly outperformed all the three configurations in PMA (raw, positional, and raw + positional data) ($p < 0.01$ also in an ANOVA test).

Although the EMA-based ATS system outperformed the PMA-based system in our experiment, this finding does not negate the merits of PMA technology. Since PMA has shown the abilities of reaching a sufficiently good level in ATS (Gonzalez et al., 2014, 2017a,b; Cheah et al., 2018). Therefore, it is still a good fit for SSI application.

In this study, we focused on the comparison of PMA and EMA, and only tongue tip motion was used for ATS performance. Other studies in literature that have incorporated lip motion and other tongue flesh point motion have achieved high performance for PMA-based ATS (Gonzalez et al., 2014, 2017a,b; Cheah et al., 2018). In addition, this study used on MCD as the ATS performance measure. While MCD is a widely used measure for ATS performance, it does not fully represent the vocal quality of the resulting speech. Other acoustic measures including band aperiodicities distortion (BAP) (Morise, 2016), root mean square error of fundamental frequencies (F0-RMSE), and voiced/unvoiced (V/UV) error rate, as well as listening tests are needed to truly assess the differences of PMA and EMA which has not been conducted in the current stage of this study as explained.

Although the subjects were age- and gender-matched in the two groups for comparison (PMA vs EMA) with the same protocol (stimuli and data size), they were different subjects. Indeed, the PMA and EMA systems were located in two different research laboratories, and they could not be placed at a same location for this study. Because the data were collected by two different teams and with different subjects for the EMA and PMA, there could likely be variations in the outcome of the study between the datasets. This issue will be resolved in the future study where the same subjects will use both devices and the same operators will supervise the data collection sessions.

5 Conclusion and Future Work

In this study, we compared the ATS performance between a PMA-based tongue motion tracking device and a commercially available EMA (NDI Wave). We found both the raw magnetic signals and transformed positional signals acquired from PMA have similar ATS performance. Although we found that PMA-based system did not perform as well as the EMA-based system in this single-tracer comparison, PMA still has great potential for SSI application, because it is wireless, affordable, portable, and easy to use. Future work will verify these findings using a larger data set (both EMA and PMA) collected from the same speakers, and further improve the PMA measurement accuracy as well as the localization approach that converts raw magnetic signals to positional data.

Acknowledgments

This work was supported by the National Institutes of Health (NIH) under award number R03DC013990 and by the American Speech-Language-Hearing Foundation through a New Century Scholar Research Grant. We also thank Dr. Maysam Ghovanloo and the volunteering participants.

References

Martín Abadi, Paul Barham, Jianmin Chen, Zhifeng Chen, Andy Davis, Jeffrey Dean, Matthieu Devin, Sanjay Ghemawat, Geoffrey Irving, Michael Isard, et al. 2016. Tensorflow: A System for Large-Scale Machine Learning. In *12th USENIX Symposium on Operating Systems Design and Implementation (OSDI'16)*, pages 265–283.

Byron J Bailey, Jonas T Johnson, and Shawn D Newlands. 2006. *Head & Neck Surgery–Otolaryngology*, volume 1. Lippincott Williams & Wilkins.

David R Baraff. 1994. Artificial Larynx. US Patent 5,326,349.

Jeffrey J Berry. 2011. Accuracy of the NDI Wave Speech Research System. *Journal of Speech, Language, and Hearing Research*, pages 1295–1301.

Florent Bocquelet, Thomas Hueber, Laurent Girin, Christophe Savariaux, and Blaise Yvert. 2016. Real-Time Control of an Articulatory-Based Speech Synthesizer for Brain Computer Interfaces. *PLoS computational biology*, 12(11):e1005119.

Beiming Cao, Myungjong Kim, J van Santen, T Mau, and J Wang. 2018. Articulation-to-Speech Synthesis Using Articulatory Flesh Point Sensors Orientation Information. In *Proc. INTERSPEECH*, pages 3152–3156.

Lam Aun Cheah, James M Gilbert, José A González, Phil D Green, Stephen R Ell, Roger K Moore, and Ed Holdsworth. 2018. A Wearable Silent Speech Interface based on Magnetic Sensors with Motion-Artefact Removal. pages 56–62.

Tamás Gábor Csapó, Tamás Grósz, Gábor Gosztolya, László Tóth, and Alexandra Markó. 2017. DNN-Based Ultrasound-to-Speech Conversion for a Silent Speech Interface. *Proc. Interspeech 2017*, pages 3672–3676.

Bruce Denby, Tanja Schultz, Kiyoshi Honda, Thomas Hueber, Jim M Gilbert, and Jonathan S Brumberg. 2010. Silent Speech Interfaces. *Speech Communication*, 52(4):270–287.

Lorenz Diener, Sebastian Bredehoeft, and Tanja Schultz. 2018. A comparison of EMG-to-Speech Conversion for Isolated and Continuous Speech. In *Speech Communication; 13th ITG-Symposium*, pages 1–5. VDE.

Sharon Glennen and Denise C DeCoste. 1997. *The Handbook of Augmentative and Alternative Communication*. Cengage Learning.

Jose A Gonzalez, Lam A Cheah, Jie Bai, Stephen R Ell, James M Gilbert, Roger K Moore, and Phil D Green. 2014. Analysis of Phonetic Similarity in a Silent Speech Interface Based on Permanent Magnetic Articulography. In *Proc. INTERSPEECH*, pages 1018–1022.

Jose A Gonzalez, Lam A Cheah, Angel M Gomez, Phil D Green, James M Gilbert, Stephen R Ell, Roger K Moore, and Ed Holdsworth. 2017a. Direct Speech Reconstruction from Articulatory Sensor Data by Machine Learning. *IEEE/ACM Transactions on Audio, Speech, and Language Processing*, 25(12):2362–2374.

Jose A Gonzalez, Lam A Cheah, Phil D Green, James M Gilbert, Stephen R Ell, Roger K Moore, and Ed Holdsworth. 2017b. Evaluation of a Silent Speech Interface Based on Magnetic Sensing and Deep Learning for a Phonetically Rich Vocabulary. *Proc. Interspeech 2017*, pages 3986–3990.

John C Gower. 1975. Generalized Procrustes Analysis. *Psychometrika*, 40(1):33–51.

Melvin Hyman. 1955. An Experimental Study of Artificial-Larynx and Esophageal Speech. *Journal of Speech and Hearing Disorders*, 20(3):291–299.

Myungjong Kim, Beiming Cao, Ted Mau, and Jun Wang. 2017. Speaker-Independent Silent Speech Recognition from Flesh-Point Articulatory Movements Using an LSTM Neural Network. *IEEE/ACM Transactions on Audio, Speech and Language Processing (TASLP)*, 25(12):2323–2336.

Myungjong Kim, Nordine Sebkhi, Beiming Cao, Maysam Ghovanloo, and Jun Wang. 2018. Preliminary Test of a Wireless Magnetic Tongue Tracking System for Silent Speech Interface. In *2018 IEEE Biomedical Circuits and Systems Conference (BioCAS)*, pages 1–4. IEEE.

Diederik P Kingma and Jimmy Ba. 2014. Adam: A Method for Stochastic Optimization. *arXiv preprint arXiv:1412.6980*.

Anne Laumann, Jaimee Holbrook, Julia Minocha, Diane Rowles, Beatrice Nardone, Dennis West, Jeonghee Kim, Joy Bruce, Elliot Roth, and Maysam Ghovanloo. 2015. Safety and Efficacy of Medically Performed Tongue Piercing in People with Tetraplegia for Use with Tongue-Operated Assistive Technology. *Topics in Spinal Cord Injury Rehabilitation*, 21(1):61–76.

Ted Mau. 2010. Diagnostic Evaluation and Management of Hoarseness. *Medical Clinics*, 94(5):945–960.

Ted Mau, Joseph Muhlestein, Sean Callahan, and Roger W Chan. 2012. Modulating Phonation Through Alteration of Vocal Fold Medial Surface Contour. *The Laryngoscope*, 122(9):2005–2014.

J. Mertl, E. kov, and B. epov. 2018. Quality of Life of Patients After Total Laryngectomy: the Struggle Against Stigmatization and Social Exclusion Using Speech Synthesis. *Disability and Rehabilitation: Assistive Technology*, 13(4):342–352.

Masanori Morise. 2015. CheapTrick, A Spectral Envelope Estimator for High-Quality Speech Synthesis. *Speech Communication*, 67:1–7.

Masanori Morise. 2016. D4C, A Band-Aperiodicity Estimator for High-Quality Speech Synthesis. *Speech Communication*, 84:57–65.

Yoshitaka Nakajima, Hideki Kashioka, Kiyohiro Shikano, and Nick Campbell. 2003. Non-Audible Murmur Recognition Input Interface Using Stethoscopic Microphone Attached to the Skin. In *2003 IEEE International Conference on Acoustics, Speech, and Signal Processing, 2003. Proceedings.(ICASSP'03).*, volume 5, pages 708–711. IEEE.

Joanne Robbins, Hilda B Fisher, Eric C Blom, and Mark I Singer. 1984. A Comparative Acoustic Study of Normal, Esophageal, and Tracheoesophageal Speech Production. *Journal of Speech and Hearing disorders*, 49(2):202–210.

Paul W Schönle, Klaus Gräbe, Peter Wenig, Jörg Höhne, Jörg Schrader, and Bastian Conrad. 1987. Electromagnetic Articulography: Use of Alternating Magnetic Fields for Tracking Movements of Multiple Points Inside and Outside the Vocal Tract. *Brain and Language*, 31(1):26–35.

Nordine Sebkhi, Dhyey Desai, Mohammad Islam, Jun Lu, Kimberly Wilson, and Maysam Ghovanloo. 2017. Multimodal Speech Capture System for Speech Rehabilitation and Learning. *IEEE Transactions on Biomedical Engineering*, 64(11):2639–2649.

Yana Yunusova, Jordan R Green, and Antje Mefferd. 2009. Accuracy Assessment for AG500, Electromagnetic Articulograph. *Journal of Speech, Language, and Hearing Research*, pages 547–555.

Speech-based Estimation of Bulbar Regression in Amyotrophic Lateral Sclerosis

Alan Wisler[1], Kristin Teplansky[1,2], Jordan R. Green[3], Yana Yunusova[4], Thomas F. Campbell[2], Daragh Heitzman[5], Jun Wang[1,2]
[1]Speech Disorders & Technology Lab, Department of Bioengineering
[2]Callier Center for Communication Disorders
University of Texas at Dallas, Richardson, TX, USA
[3] Department of Communication Sciences and Disorders
MGH Institute of Health Professions, Boston, MA, USA
[4] Department of Speech-Language Pathology, University of Toronto, Toronto, ON, Canada
[5] MDA/ALS Center, Texas Neurology, Dallas, TX, USA

Abstract

Amyotrophic Lateral Sclerosis (ALS) is a progressive neurological disease that leads to degeneration of motor neurons and, as a result, inhibits the ability of the brain to control muscle movements. Monitoring the progression of ALS is of fundamental importance due to the wide variability in disease outlook that exists across patients. This progression is typically tracked using the ALS functional rating scale - revised (ALSFRS-R), which is the current clinical assessment of a patient's level of functional impairment including speech and other motor tasks. In this paper, we investigated automatic estimation of the ALSFRS-R bulbar subscore from acoustic and articulatory movement samples. Experimental results demonstrated the AFSFRS-R bulbar subscore can be predicted from speech samples, which has clinical implication for automatic monitoring of the disease progression of ALS using speech information.

1 Introduction

Amyotrophic Lateral Sclerosis (ALS, also known as Lou Gehrig's disease) is a progressive neurological disease that destroys nerve cells and inhibits the normal voluntary motor function of the affected individual. The progression of this disease rapidly limits the patient's ability to perform normal daily tasks such as walking, speaking, and eventually even breathing. Although there is currently no cure for ALS, early detection and accurate tracking of disease progression is crucial to the planning of treatment strategies and therapeutic intervention (Kiernan et al., 2011). The currently used clinical measure for the disease progression is the patient self-reported ALSFRS-R score, which estimates the degree of functional impairment across motor tasks such as speaking and walking, as well as common daily tasks such as getting dressed and climbing the stairs (Cedarbaum et al., 1999).

ALSFRS-R has a collection of 12 questions, with a total score ranging from 0 to 48, which is composed of three factors: bulbar functions, fine and gross motor functions, and respiratory function (Franchignoni et al., 2013). Bulbar functions include speaking, salivating, and swallowing. The efficacy of the ALSFRS-R for measuring motor-function and levels of self-sufficiency of individuals with ALS has been thoroughly demonstrated. The ALSFRS-R has shown high inter-rater reliability, test-retest reliability, and internal consistency (Cedarbaum and Stambler, 1997; Brinkmann et al., 1997). Additionally, the ALSFRS-R is highly correlated with the clinical stage of ALS (Balendra et al., 2014) and has been shown to be a useful predictor of patient survival (Magnus et al., 2002). Despite the utility and reliability of the ALSFRS-R, it is only able to quantify specific degradations in motor function along a five point scale. As such, it lacks the resolution to capture more subtle changes in motor function that can be observed through instrumentation-based measures (Allison et al., 2017).

Recently, there has been a surge of research using speech analytics to detect and track a range of neurological diseases such as Parkinson's (Orozco-Arroyave et al., 2016a,b; Hsu et al., 2017; Benba et al., 2015) and ALS (An et al., 2018; ill; Norel et al., 2018; Wang et al., 2016a,b, 2018). Efforts towards tracking disease progression in this area have typically focused on the estimation of speech specific measures such as speech intelligibility (Berisha et al., 2013; Kim et al., 2015),

Proceedings of the Eighth Workshop on Speech and Language Processing for Assistive Technologies, pages 24–31
Minneapolis, Minnesota, USA ©2019 Association for Computational Linguistics

speaking rate (Jiao et al., 2016; Martens et al., 2015), or severity (Tu et al., 2017; Asgari and Shafran, 2010). While these efforts have shown success in the ability to objectively measure functional changes directly related to speech, whether speech can be used to measure functional impairment along other tasks in ALS remains largely unexplored.

In this paper we sought to address this question by examining how well speech and articulation data can predict the ALSFRS-R bulbar subscore (ranges from 0 to 12). The long-term goal of this research is to develop objective measures for broad level motor function. At this early stage, we focused on the bulbar score first. To our knowledge, this paper is the first to predict ALSFRS-R (bulbar) score directly from speech information. Two regression models, a simple linear ridge regression model and a machine learning algorithm (support vector machine), were used in the regression analysis.

2 Data Collection

2.1 Participants

Sixty-six speakers diagnosed with ALS at early-onset participated in this study at up to four data collection sessions with an interval of four to six months. At each session, participants or caregivers completed the ALSFRS-R, which included the bulbar subscore. Speech intelligibility (percentage of understandable words, judged by listeners) and speaking rate (words produced per minute) were assessed by a speech-language pathologist using the Sentence Intelligibility Test (SIT) software (Dorsey et al., 2007). Intelligible speaking rate, called communication efficiency, was also calculated, which is the percentage of understandable words per minute (speech intelligibility × speaking rate) (Yorkston and Beukelman, 1981). The whole data set was used for the basic correlation analysis between ALSFRS-R and speech performance measures, while the data from 28 participants were used for regression analysis. This subset includes 15 male and 13 female participants, whose age averaged 57.3 years with a standard deviation of 10.7 years.

2.2 Stimuli and Procedure

The participants were asked to produce 20 sentences in a fixed order, such as *I need some assistance* and *call me back when you can*. A complete list of the stimuli used for data collection is included in the Appendix. The sentences were selected because they are commonly used in augmentative and alternative communication (AAC) devices (Beukelman et al., 1984). All speech stimuli were presented on a TV screen in front of the participants. The stimuli were repeated for a total of four recordings at the participants habitual speaking rate among other speech tasks.

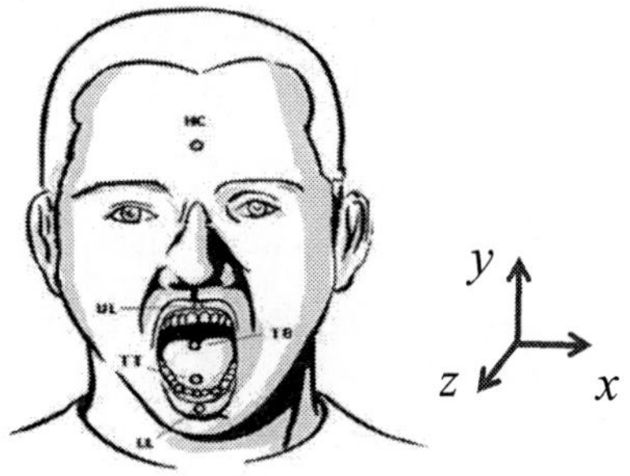

Figure 1: Sensor locations for the Wave system

The NDI Wave System (Northern Digital Inc., Waterloo, Canada) was used to collect articulatory movement data with an accuracy of 0.5 mm (Berry, 2011). An optimal four sensor set-up (Wang et al., 2016c) was used to collect articulatory data from the tongue tip (TT, 5 mm from apex), tongue back (TB, 10 mm from TT), upper lip (UL, vermillion border) and lower lip (LL, vermillion border). The sensors were attached using nontoxic dental glue (PeriAcryl 90, GluStitch) or medical tape. A lightweight helmet with a 6 degree-of-freedom sensor served as a point of head reference. Prior to the start of each data collection session, the speakers had 3-5 minutes to adapt to the wired sensors prior to formal data collection. In this paper, we used x, y, and z to represent lateral, vertical, and anterior-posterior movements, respectively. A visual depiction of the sensor locations and coordinate system is displayed in Figure 1. To capture acoustic signals simultaneously, a Shure Microflex microphone with a sampling rate of 22kHz was positioned approximately 15 cm from each speaker's mouth.

2.3 Data Processing

Head rotation and translation movements were removed from articulatory data prior to analysis. A low pass filter of 15hz was applied to remove noise (Wang et al., 2016c). SMASH (Green et al., 2013a), a Matlab based software, was used segment the time-matched articulatory and acoustic data into individual phrase samples.

2.4 Relationship between ALSFRS-R scores and speech performance measures

In this section, we evaluated the relationship between traditional speech metrics, such as speaking rate and speech intelligibility, and ALSFRS-R scores. Because speech represents only a small component of the broad motor function assessed by the ALSFRS-R, we not only compared the relationship between speech and the ALSFRS-R as a whole, but also at the Bulbar subscore, which reflects the portion of the ALSFRS-R related to speaking, salivating and swallowing.

There are several important factors to consider when evaluating the relationship between these measures and ALSFRS-R score. First, neither the speech metrics nor the ALSFRS-R scores being compared are perfect measures of the underlying decline in motor function that they attempt to quantify. Speaking rate is highly sensitive to natural deviation between speakers and compensatory strategies that can mask changes in motor function (Green et al., 2013b). Speech intelligibility suffers from ceiling and floor effects that prevent it from tracking disease progression outside of a fixed severity range (Yorkston and Beukelman, 1981). Second, because the ALSFRS-R measures each motor component along a 5-point scale it cannot capture subtle changes to motor control that occur between points on this scale. Despite this limitation, the ALSFRS-R has been proven reliable in test-retest analysis (Cedarbaum and Stambler, 1997) and correlates highly with the clinical stage of individuals with ALS (Balendra et al., 2014).

Figure 2 displays the relationship between speech intelligibility, speaking rate, and intelligible speaking rate (ISR) and the ALSFRS-R bulbar subscore for participants in our data set. Although all three scatter plots show a correlation between the measures of speech and the ALSFRS-R bulbar subscore, there exists significant variability in the ALSFRS-R that cannot be explained by the measures of speech. This is particularly true of intelligibility, where participants could score as low as 4/12 of the ALSFRS-R bulbar subscore, while maintaining near-perfect intelligibility. Among the three speech measures, ISR had the highest correlation with ALSFRS Bulbar subscore.

To better understand the relationship between these speech measures and the different components of the ALSFRS-R, we performed a correlation analysis between three measures of speech intelligibility, speaking rate, and ISR, and three ALSFRS-R component scores (Table 1). The three component scores were (a) the total score, which provides a broad assessment of motor function, (b) the bulbar subscore, which includes functions of motor control most closely related to speech including assessment of speaking, swallowing and salivating, and (c) the non-bulbar component, which is the difference between the total ALSFRS-R score and the bulbar subscore. This analysis found a strong correlation between all three measures of speech and the Bulbar subscore with all correlations between 0.5 and 0.7 and all p-values less than 10^{-6}. Although there exists a statistically significant relationship between each of the speech measures and the total ALSFRS-R score, this significance disappears if the bulbar component is removed. Therefore this relationship is simply more evidence of the speech measures ability to track the bulbar component.

3 Methods

As mentioned earlier, this analysis was based on a subset of twenty eight participants from the previously described data set whose speech data has been manually parsed for automatic processing. Fifteen of the patients only made a single visit, six made two visits, five made three visits, and only two made the full four visits. Though the number of samples collected for each patient is usually 80 per session, some of the participants were not able to complete all of the recording tasks. In these cases predictions were made based on the reduced set of samples that were available.

3.1 Acoustic Features

The acoustic features used in this paper were based on the frame-level Mel-frequency cepstral coefficients (MFCCs). Although MFCCs were originally popularized due to their effectiveness in automatic speech recognition systems, they have recently seen increasing usage in a range of other speech assessment tasks, including the detection of motor speech disorders like Parkinson's disease (Benba et al., 2015). As the mel cepstrum encodes spectral magnitude information related to the shape of the vocal tract, MFCC's can capture articulatory changes resulting from conditions like

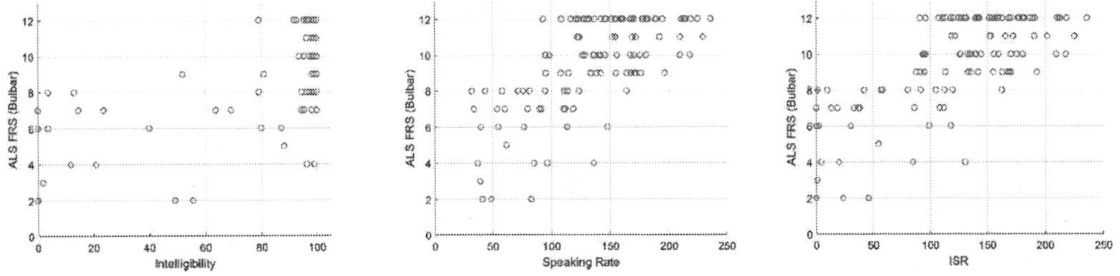

(a) Intelligibility (b) Speaking Rate (c) Intelligible Speaking Rate

Figure 2: Scatter plots depicting the relationship between the three speech metrics and ALSFRS-R Bulbar subscore for each participant & recording session in the data set.

	ALSFRS-R		ALSFRS-R (Bulbar)		ALSFRS-R (non-Bulbar)	
	Correlation	p-value	Correlation	p-value	Correlation	p-value
Intelligibility	0.1960	0.0366	0.5840	$< 10^{-6}$	0.0005	0.9954
Speaking Rate	0.2419	0.0095	0.6422	$< 10^{-6}$	0.0286	0.7625
ISR	0.2331	0.0126	0.6957	$< 10^{-6}$	0.0002	0.9981

Table 1: Correlations between the speech measures and ALSFRS-R overall, bulbar, and non-bulbar scores.

depression (Williamson et al., 2014) or dysarthria (Fraile et al., 2008). For each frame we extracted 14 MFCCs, along with their first and second temporal derivatives ΔMFCC and ΔΔMFCC. From these 42 variables across time, we calculate 3 different summary statistics, mean, standard deviation and pairwise variability yielding a total of 126 features.

3.2 Articulatory Features

For a specific sensor, we have three positional arrays $\mathbf{x} = [x_1, ..., x_N]$, $\mathbf{y} = [y_1, ..., y_N$, and $\mathbf{z} = [z_1, ..., z_N$ corresponding to dimensions x, y, and z. For any index $i \in [1, .., N-1]$, we can calculate the corresponding distance traveled as

$$d_i = \sqrt{(x_{i+1} - x_i)^2 + (y_{i+1} - y_i)^2 + (z_{i+1} - z_i)^2} \quad (1)$$

and form the corresponding distance matrix

$$\mathbf{D} = [d_1, ..., d_{N-1}]. \quad (2)$$

This distance matrix forms the basis for the articulation features used in this paper. From $\mathbf{D}$, we extracted eight summary statistics: mean, standard deviation, skewness, kurtosis, maximum, minimum, range, and pairwise variability. In addition to these baseline features, we considered three procedures for normalizing the feature based on measurements of the overall distance trajectory. The first normalization procedure was dividing the features by the overall distance traveled $\sum \mathbf{D}$, in order to control for the distance of the overall articulation motion which was heavily dependent on the specific phrase being produced. The second and third normalization procedures attempted to control for the size of each individual's articulation motion space, the first by normalizing between the maximum overall distance between any two points in $(\mathbf{x}, \mathbf{y}, \mathbf{z})$. The second was forming a convex hull around the articulation path and normalizing based on the volume of the resulting hull. Combining the 8 different statistics and four normalization methods (including no normalization) with the four different sensors (Tongue-tip, tongue-back,lower lip and upper lip) yielded a total of 128 features.

To illustrate how these articulatory features might help assess motor function for different individuals, we plotted the articulation data from two different patients on opposite ends of the severity spectrum in our dataset (Figure 3). The first sample was from participant DA001 on his/her first visit. This participant experienced minimal decline in their speaking abilities and scored a perfect 12/12 on the ALSFRS-R bulbar subscore. The second sample was drawn from patient DA016 on her second visit, where she had a severe speech decline already scoring only 3/12 points on the Bulbar subsection. Figure 3 displays the tongue-tip articulation tracks for the two participants, along with a box plot comparing the distribution of the distance values between points

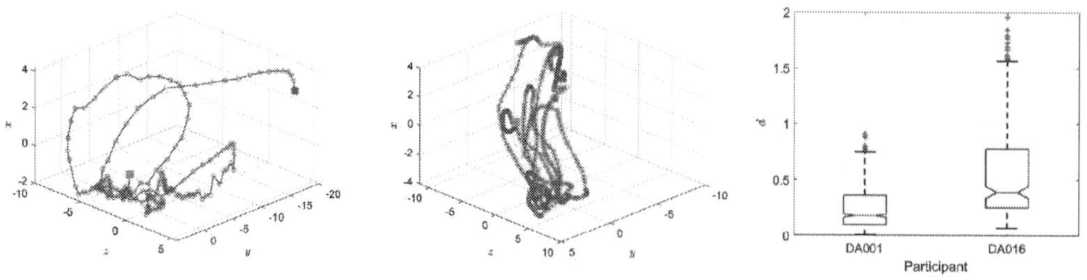

(a) DA001 Articulation Plot (b) DA016 Articulation Plot (c) Box Plot

Figure 3: Articulation plots for two participants (a) DA001 (normal speech) and (b) DA016 (severe speech deficit) while speaking the phrase "I need to see a doctor", along with (c) a box plot comparing the distributions of distances between adjacent points in the articulation track for each participant. In the articulation plots, the starting point of the articulatory motion is marked with a red cross and the end is marked with a green square.

for each participant. As shown in Figures 3a and 3b, participant DA016 has a significantly reduced articulation space relative to DA001, where DA001's space had a volume that almost doubled DA016's (335.96 vs. 181.55). Additionally, the box plot in Figure 3c shows a stark difference between the distribution of pairwise distances across the two participants. The distances for participant DA016 are significantly lower on average than DA016, indicating a pronounced reduction in the speed of articulation.

3.3 Regression Analysis

The regression analysis conducted in this experiment began with the 3959 $\times$ 254 dimension feature matrix extracted via the procedure outlined in the previous section. To ensure the regression model's ability to generalize to new speakers, it is evaluated by leave-one-speaker-out cross-validation. Thus at every stage of cross-validation, the model is trained using 27 participants and evaluated based on the single left-out participant. When a participant with multiple recording sessions is moved to the validation set, all sessions are moved to the validation set as a group and unique predictions are made and evaluated for each session.

All the data samples were z-scored (subtracted the mean and divided by the standard deviation) to obtain the normalized feature data. This procedure helped prevent the scale of different attributes affecting how much they contribute to the model.

Two regression models were used in this analysis, a simple ridge regression model and a support vector machine (SVM). Ridge regression is similar to ordinary least-squares regression, but utilizes an L_2 regularization term in order to better model data that is subject to multicollinearities (Hoerl and Kennard, 1970). Unlike traditional regression models that minimize observed training error, support vector regression (SVR) minimizes a generalization bound in order to ensure the model performs well on out-of-sample data (Basak et al., 2007). This factor, combined with the ability of SVMs to use non-linear kernels to model complex non-linear patterns in data, has made them widely used for both classification and regression problems. The SVMs used in this paper employed a linear kernel and were trained using the sequential minimal optimization (SMO) algorithm.

In addition to the baseline model (using all previously described acoustic and articulation features), we also tested the performance of other five feature groups, acoustic only, acoustic + lips, tongue, lips, and tongue + lips. The initial predictions were made on individual samples (phrases), and were then averaged to form a final prediction for each patient-session pair.

Two measures were used for the regression performance, root mean squared error (RMSE) and the correlation of the resulting set of predictions with the true ALSFRS-R (bulbar) scores. Low RMSE indicates that the small difference between the predicted and true ALSFRS-R values. High correlation indicates that changes in the predicted ALSFRS-R values are likely corresponding to a proportional changes in the true values.

4 Results

The results for each of the six feature group and two regression models are displayed in terms of both RMSE and correlation in Figure 4. The high-

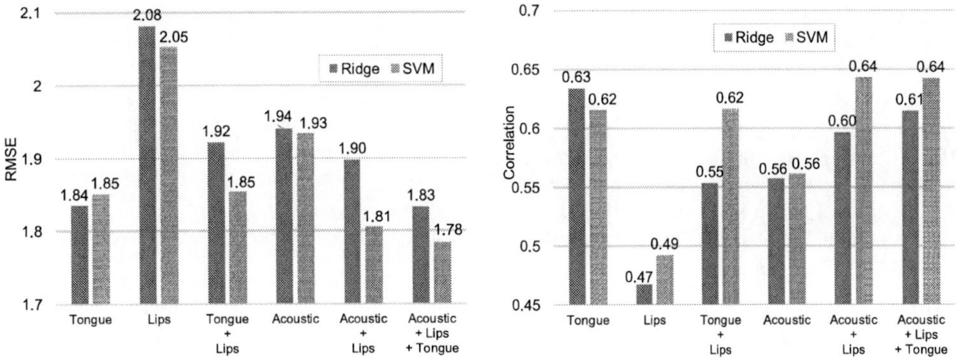

(a) RMSE

(b) Correlation

Figure 4: Bar graphs describing the performance of Ridge (blue) and SVM (orange) models across the six feature groupings described along the x-axis in terms of both root mean-squared error and correlation.

est performance was achieved by the SVR model using acoustic data along with all articulatory motion data (RMSE $= 1.78$, $r = 0.64$).

Figure 4 indicated a few interesting findings. First, we found that the models trained on both the articulation motion data and the acoustic data tended to outperform either grouping by itself. This is consistent with the literature on both ISR prediction (Wang et al., 2016b, 2018) and ALS early detection (Wang et al., 2016a), which have shown the performance benefits of adding articulatory data to acoustic models.

In addition, the performance on data from tongue or lips separately shows that the tongue sensors were significantly more powerful than lips for predicting ALSFRS-R scores when viewed in isolation, which is not surprising, as the tongue is the primary articulator. Wang and colleagues also found tongue information outperformed lip information in predicting intelligible speaking rate for ALS (Wang et al., 2018).

Interestingly, when comparing the performances between the "Acoustic+Lips" group and the "All Features" group, we found that the addition of the tongue data (on top of acoustic and lip motion data) did not significantly improve the performance. Further studies, however, are required to verify this finding with a deeper analysis on the performance of additional tongue information on top of acoustic and lip information. Future research should investigate the degree to which non-invasive video-based measures of lip motion can be substituted for the more traditional motion-sensors. This finding supports the idea that a mobile app for recording speech and lip motion (via a webcam) would be beneficial for future home-based data collection from patients.

Finally, when comparing the performance of the two regression models that were tested, SVM tended to perform slightly better than the ridge regression models. The lone exception to this was in the case of tongue-only articulation data, where the ridge regression model slightly outperformed the SVM. Future work will involve more complicated models such as convolutional neural networks (CNNs), which have recently shown potential in ALS early detection (An et al., 2018).

5 Conclusion

This paper explored automatic estimation of the ALSFRS-R bulbar score from speech information, where both acoustic and articulatory motion data collected during speech production were used. Two regression models, support vector regression and ridge regression, were applied on six different feature groups/sets. The highest performance was achieved by the SVR model using acoustic data along with all articulatory motion data. To our knowledge, for the first time, we demonstrated the feasibility of automatic prediction of ALSFRS-R bulbar score from speech samples. Future research on this topic will focus on the degree to which non-speech information can be included to predict ALS motor function decline more broadly.

Acknowledgments

This work was supported by the National Institutes of Health (NIH) under award numbers R01DC013547 and R03DC013990.

References

Kristen M Allison, Yana Yunusova, Thomas F Campbell, Jun Wang, James D Berry, and Jordan R Green. 2017. The diagnostic utility of patient-report and speech-language pathologists' ratings for detecting the early onset of bulbar symptoms due to als. *Amyotrophic Lateral Sclerosis and Frontotemporal Degeneration*, 18(5-6):358–366.

KwangHoon An, Myungjong Kim, Kristin Teplansky, Jordan R Green, Thomas F Campbell, Yana Yunusova, Daragh Heitzman, and Jun Wang. 2018. Automatic early detection of amyotrophic lateral sclerosis from intelligible speech using convolutional neural networks. *Proc. Interspeech 2018*, pages 1913–1917.

Meysam Asgari and Izhak Shafran. 2010. Predicting severity of parkinson's disease from speech. In *2010 Annual International Conference of the IEEE Engineering in Medicine and Biology*, pages 5201–5204. IEEE.

Rubika Balendra, Ashley Jones, Naheed Jivraj, Catherine Knights, Catherine M Ellis, Rachel Burman, Martin R Turner, P Nigel Leigh, Christopher E Shaw, and Ammar Al-Chalabi. 2014. Estimating clinical stage of amyotrophic lateral sclerosis from the als functional rating scale. *Amyotrophic Lateral Sclerosis and Frontotemporal Degeneration*, 15(3-4):279–284.

Debasish Basak, Srimanta Pal, and Dipak Chandra Patranabis. 2007. Support vector regression. *Neural Information Processing-Letters and Reviews*, 11(10):203–224.

Achraf Benba, Abdelilah Jilbab, and Ahmed Hammouch. 2015. Detecting patients with parkinson's disease using mel frequency cepstral coefficients and support vector machines. *International Journal on Electrical Engineering and Informatics*, 7(2):297.

Visar Berisha, Rene Utianski, and Julie Liss. 2013. Towards a clinical tool for automatic intelligibility assessment. In *2013 IEEE International Conference on Acoustics, Speech and Signal Processing*, pages 2825–2828. IEEE.

Jeffrey J Berry. 2011. Accuracy of the NDI wave speech research system. *Journal of Speech, Language, and Hearing Research*, 54:1295–1301.

David R. Beukelman, Kathryn M. Yorkston, Miguel Poblete, and Carlos Naranjo. 1984. Frequency of word occurrence in communication samples produced by adult communication aid users. *Journal of Speech and Hearing Disorders*, 49:360–367.

James R Brinkmann, Patricia Andres, Michelle Mendoza, and Mohammed Sanjak. 1997. Guidelines for the use and performance of quantitative outcome measures in ALS clinical trials. *Journal of the Nneurological Sciences*, 147(1):97–111.

Jesse M Cedarbaum and Nancy Stambler. 1997. Performance of the amyotrophic lateral sclerosis functional rating scale (alsfrs) in multicenter clinical trials. *Journal of the Neurological Sciences*, 152:s1–9.

Jesse M Cedarbaum, Nancy Stambler, Errol Malta, Cynthia Fuller, Dana Hilt, Barbara Thurmond, Arline Nakanishi, BDNF ALS Study Group, 1A complete listing of the BDNF Study Group, et al. 1999. The alsfrs-r: a revised als functional rating scale that incorporates assessments of respiratory function. *Journal of the Neurological Sciences*, 169(1-2):13–21.

Matt Dorsey, Kathryn Yorkston, David Beukelman, and Mark Hakel. 2007. Speech intelligibility test for windows.

Rubén Fraile, Juan Ignacio Godino-Llorente, Nicolás Sáenz-Lechón, Víctor Osma-Ruiz, and Pedro Gómez Vilda. 2008. Use of cepstrum-based parameters for automatic pathology detection on speech-analysis of performance and theoretical justification. volume 1, pages 85–91.

Franco Franchignoni, Gabriele Mora, Andrea Giordano, Paolo Volanti, and Adriano Chiò. 2013. Evidence of multidimensionality in the alsfrs-r scale: a critical appraisal on its measurement properties using rasch analysis. *J Neurol Neurosurg Psychiatry*, 84(12):1340–1345.

Jordan R Green, Jun Wang, and David L Wilson. 2013a. SMASH: a tool for articulatory data processing and analysis. In *Interspeech*, pages 1331–1335. IEEE.

Jordan R Green, Yana Yunusova, Mili S Kuruvilla, Jun Wang, Gary L Pattee, Lori Synhorst, Lorne Zinman, and James D Berry. 2013b. Bulbar and speech motor assessment in als: Challenges and future directions. *Amyotrophic Lateral Sclerosis and Frontotemporal Degeneration*, 14(7-8):494–500.

Arthur E Hoerl and Robert W Kennard. 1970. Ridge regression: Biased estimation for nonorthogonal problems. *Technometrics*, 12(1):55–67.

Sih-Chiao Hsu, Yishan Jiao, Megan J McAuliffe, Visar Berisha, Ruey-Meei Wu, and Erika S Levy. 2017. Acoustic and perceptual speech characteristics of native mandarin speakers with parkinson's disease. *The Journal of the Acoustical Society of America*, 141(3):EL293–EL299.

Yishan Jiao, Ming Tu, Visar Berisha, and Julie Liss. 2016. Online speaking rate estimation using recurrent neural networks. In *2016 IEEE International Conference on Acoustics, Speech and Signal Processing (ICASSP)*, pages 5245–5249. IEEE.

Matthew C Kiernan, Steve Vucic, Benjamin C Cheah, Martin R Turner, Andrew Eisen, Orla Hardiman, James R Burrell, and Margaret C Zoing. 2011. Amyotrophic lateral sclerosis. *The lancet*, 377(9769):942–955.

Myung Jong Kim, Younggwan Kim, and Hoirin Kim. 2015. Automatic intelligibility assessment of dysarthric speech using phonologically-structured sparse linear model. *IEEE/ACM Transactions on Audio, Speech, and Language Processing*, 23(4):694–704.

T Magnus, M Beck, R Giess, I Puls, M Naumann, and KV Toyka. 2002. Disease progression in amyotrophic lateral sclerosis: predictors of survival. *Muscle & Nerve: Official Journal of the American Association of Electrodiagnostic Medicine*, 25(5):709–714.

Heidi Martens, Tomas Dekens, Gwen Van Nuffelen, Lukas Latacz, Werner Verhelst, and Marc De Bodt. 2015. Automated speech rate measurement in dysarthria. *Journal of Speech, Language, and Hearing Research*, 58(3):698–712.

Raquel Norel, Mary Pietrowicz, Carla Agurto, Shay Rishoni, and Guillermo Cecchi. 2018. Detection of amyotrophic lateral sclerosis (ALS) via acoustic analysis. In *Proc. Interspeech*, pages 377–381.

JR Orozco-Arroyave, F Hönig, JD Arias-Londoño, JF Vargas-Bonilla, K Daqrouq, S Skodda, J Rusz, and E Nöth. 2016a. Automatic detection of parkinson's disease in running speech spoken in three different languages. *The Journal of the Acoustical Society of America*, 139(1):481–500.

Juan Rafael Orozco-Arroyave, JC Vdsquez-Correa, Florian Hönig, Julián D Arias-Londoño, JF Vargas-Bonilla, Sabine Skodda, Jan Rusz, and E Noth. 2016b. Towards an automatic monitoring of the neurological state of parkinson's patients from speech. In *2016 IEEE International Conference on Acoustics, Speech and Signal Processing (ICASSP)*, pages 6490–6494. IEEE.

Ming Tu, Visar Berisha, and Julie Liss. 2017. Objective assessment of pathological speech using distribution regression. In *2017 IEEE International Conference on Acoustics, Speech and Signal Processing (ICASSP)*, pages 5050–5054. IEEE.

Jun Wang, Prasanna V Kothalkar, Beiming Cao, and Daragh Heitzman. 2016a. Towards automatic detection of amyotrophic lateral sclerosis from speech acoustic and articulatory samples. In *Interspeech*, pages 1195–1199.

Jun Wang, Prasanna V Kothalkar, Myungjong Kim, Andrea Bandini, Beiming Cao, Yana Yunusova, Thomas F Campbell, Daragh Heitzman, and Jordan R Green. 2018. Automatic prediction of intelligible speaking rate for individuals with ALS from speech acoustic and articulatory samples. *International journal of speech-language pathology*, 20(6):669–679.

Jun Wang, Prasanna V Kothalkar, Myungjong Kim, Yana Yunusova, Thomas F Campbell, Daragh Heitzman, and Jordan R Green. 2016b. Predicting intelligible speaking rate in individuals with amyotrophic lateral sclerosis from a small number of speech acoustic and articulatory samples. In *Workshop on Speech and Language Processing for Assistive Technologies*, volume 2016, page 91. NIH Public Access.

Jun Wang, Ashok Samal, Panying Rong, and Jordan R Green. 2016c. An optimal set of flesh points on tongue and lips for speech-movement classification. *Journal of Speech, Language, and Hearing Research*, 59(1):15–26.

James R Williamson, Thomas F Quatieri, Brian S Helfer, Gregory Ciccarelli, and Daryush D Mehta. 2014. Vocal and facial biomarkers of depression based on motor incoordination and timing. In *Proceedings of the 4th International Workshop on Audio/Visual Emotion Challenge*, pages 65–72. ACM.

Kathryn M Yorkston and David R Beukelman. 1981. Communication efficiency of dysarthric speakers as measured by sentence intelligibility and speaking rate. *Journal of Speech and Hearing Disorders*, 46(3):296–301.

Appendix

Index	Phrase
1	*I love you*
2	*Good afternoon*
3	*I changed my mind*
4	*I need some assistance*
5	*Come back again*
6	*Nice to see you*
7	*Not very good today*
8	*I need to see a doctor*
9	*I am fine*
10	*Thanks for stopping by*
11	*How are you*
12	*Call me back when you can*
13	*Great to see you again*
14	*Can I have that*
15	*This is an emergency*
16	*What are you doing*
17	*Good-bye*
18	*When will you be back*
19	*Give me one minute*
20	*I need to make an appointment*

Table 2: List of stimuli used for data collection.

A Blissymbolics Translation System

Usman Sohail
USC Institute for Creative Technologies
12015 Waterfront Dr. Playa Vista,
CA 900094, USA
msohail@usc.edu

David Traum
USC Institute for Creative Technologies
12015 Waterfront Dr. Playa Vista,
CA 900094, USA
traum@ict.usc.edu

Abstract

Blissymbolics (Bliss) is a pictographic writing system that is used by people with communication disorders. Bliss attempts to create a writing system that makes words easier to distinguish by using pictographic symbols that encapsulate meaning rather than sound, as the English alphabet does for example. Users of Bliss rely on human interpreters to use Bliss. We created a translation system from Bliss to natural English with the hopes of decreasing the reliance on human interpreters by the Bliss community. We first discuss the basic rules of Blissymbolics. Then we point out some of the challenges associated with developing computer assisted tools for Blissymbolics. Next we talk about our ongoing work in developing a translation system, including current limitations, and future work. We conclude with a set of examples showing the current capabilities of our translation system.

1 Background

An estimated 7.7% of children aged 3-17 have had a communication disorder, 44.8% of which receive no intervention services (Black et al., 2015). Blissymbolics was created to provide a tool for cognitive, and speech related communication disorders. Blissymbolics(Bliss, 1965), uses pictographic symbols to represent language as opposed to existing alphabetic writing systems in order to provide an alternate that may be easier to learn for people with low literacy.

In 1985, Muter and Johns conducted three experiments to see if ideographic symbols made it easier to extract meaning from words compared to alphabetic symbols. Their experiments showed shorter reaction times for extracting meaning from symbols of Blissymbolics than for words spelled in an unfamiliar language (Muter and Johns, 1985). Therefore Blissymbolics may be easier to learn for people with low literacy. In addition, Blissymbolics can be used without any speech, which may be useful for people with speech related communication disorders.

Although many people use Blissymbolics, they still have to rely on an interpreter to communicate with the general population. In this paper, we discuss a prototype system we developed that translates Blissymbolics utterances to English. We also discuss the future work we think is necessary for this to become feasible for mainstream use.

Blissymbolics is composed of graphic Bliss characters that form the smallest unit of meaning. There are four categories of reasoning for creating a glyph for Bliss characters illustrated in figure 1.

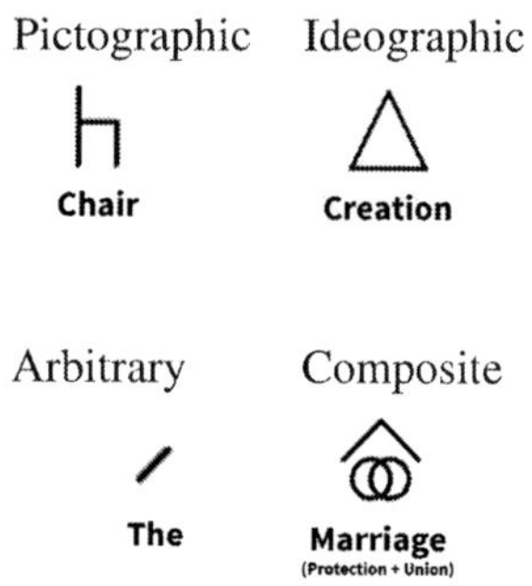

Figure 1

Bliss characters can be combined to form Bliss words with new meanings similar to the way English words can be composed of one or more letters. However, individual symbols in Bliss correspond to a morpheme, or smallest unit of meaning, unlike the phonetic correspondence of written English. In figure 2, the symbol for *house* combined with the symbol for *medical* form the word *hospital, clinic*.

Proceedings of the Eighth Workshop on Speech and Language Processing for Assistive Technologies, pages 32–36
Minneapolis, Minnesota, USA ©2019 Association for Computational Linguistics

Figure 2

2 Challenges of Blissymbolics

2.1 Encoding

Currently there is no agreed upon encoding for Bliss characters, making it difficult to develop computer assisted tools. The official Blissymbolics dictionary contains a unique 4-5 digit code associated with each Bliss character or Bliss word. This encoding scheme does not differentiate between Bliss characters and words. This is the only encoding we were able to find.

2.2 Computer Assisted Tools

Currently, users of Blissymbolics are restricted by the need for an interpreter. Although the internet has provided many tools for Blissymbolics, there has yet to be a satisfactory translation tool from Blissymbolics to natural language. Most online tools are focused on creating customized Bliss charts. For example, the chart in figure 3 about food was created using *blissonline* [1].

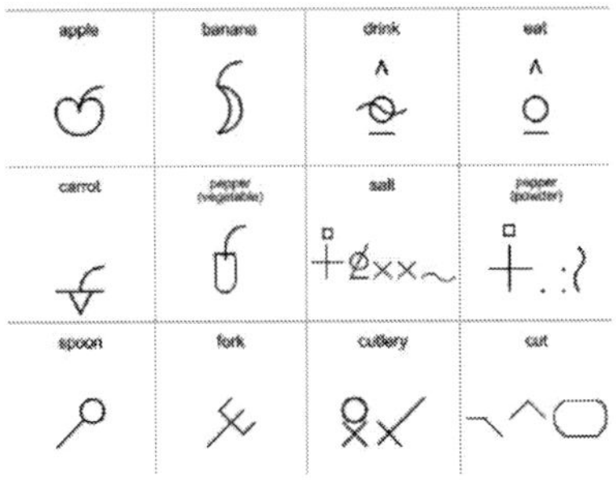

Figure 3

Bliss charts help users communicate with non-Blissymbolics users since the symbols are annotated with their translation. However, users are restricted to the number of symbols that fit on one chart and the expressiveness of Blissymbolics is reduced. Previous work has addressed the large number of symbols by dynamically changing the chart as symbols are input so that only valid options are presented to the user at each step (Netzer and Elhadad, 2006).

[1] www.blissonline.org

Attempts have been made to create a translation system from Blissymbolics to natural language. Several systems have a digital bliss chart that synthesizes speech for a given bliss word that is selected [2]. The digital nature of such devices helps increase the number of symbols that a user can access. Still, users are not able to build words up from the characters that compose them.

At the University of Dundee (Waller and Jack, 2002), a predictive translation system prototype was built using a trigram language model. The system took Blissymbols as input and output English sentences. The gloss of each Blissymbol contains one or more words of the target language. The system consulted the trigram model to find the most probable word from a given gloss. The system also looked for words that probably belonged between any two words, such as articles (which are often implied in Blissymbolics). Although the results of the system were not good enough for mainstream use, the study paved the way for Natural Language Processing techniques to be applied to Blissymbolics, and highlights some shortcomings that need to be addressed for our work.

First, the input to the prototype translation system is full Bliss words, not necessarily the characters that compose them. In the current official dictionary, there are 404 unique Bliss characters, and 4,626 unique Bliss words that are composed of one or more characters. If the system had the ability to build up words from the characters that compose them, then users would only need access to 404 unique symbols, as opposed to all symbols (characters and words).

Second, the translation system does not allow the creation of new words. The official dictionary contains words that are agreed upon by Blissymbolics International, but does not contain all possible words, or even all conjugations of those words. The Blissymbolics Fundamental Rules includes a section on building new vocabulary words, acknowledging that not all words will necessarily be built the same way by all users, and that users may want to express words that are not in the official lexicon. The rules provide an example of a word being built in a different way than the official dictionary.

For example, in Figure 4, the official spelling of teacher is composed of the characters for *person*

[2] www.tobiidynavox.com, www.minspeak.com

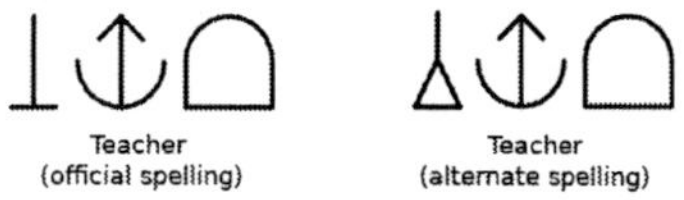

Figure 4

(non-gendered) + *giving* + *knowledge*. The fundamental rules concede that the same word should be able to be built with the symbol *female* replacing *person (non-gendered)*. Additionally, there is no official spelling for the word *cried*, although there is a word for *cry* and there is a *past action* indicator character that is made to be used as in figure 5.

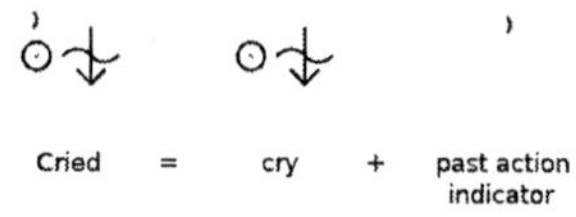

Figure 5

A translation system that could handle alternate spellings and unseen conjugations would help relax the strict spelling requirements of the official dictionary as intended by the Blissymbolics community, and increase the expressibility of the system.

3 Our Translation System

We built a translation system in Python available on github[3]. We made a few assumptions about how Blissymbolics would be used. First, we assumed that any input sequence would have a word separating token, as the Fundamental Rules of Blissymbolics dictate. Second, we used the encoding scheme found in The Official Blissymbolics Dictionary, where each Bliss symbol, word or character, is given a unique 4-5 digit numeric ID. Our translation system only accepts these IDs as input. We will need to create a graphical user interface that allows users to select the Bliss characters to input in order to make this system usable.

The work associated with building our translation system focuses on Morphological Realization, and a Language Model.

3.1 Morphological Realization

We wanted users to have the ability to express words or conjugations of existing words that are not in the Official Blissymbolics Dictionary. For now, we only applied morphological realization on recognized Bliss words, meaning only officially recognized words can be conjugated in new ways.

We used the SimpleNLG realizer (Gatt and Reiter, 2009) to conjugate Bliss words. For example, if an input Bliss character sequence had a Bliss past tense indicator, we applied the past tense realization to it. So a user could input the spelling for the bliss word translating to *cry, weep* and append the past tense indicator to the end, and get the resulting words *cried, wept.*

Currently the system is limited to morphological realization supported by SimpleNLG. There are over 40 morphological relationships included in Blissymbolics. Each relationship needs its own realizing mechanism, not all of which can be found in SimpleNLG. For example, there is a Bliss character *combine* meant to combine two concepts found in Bliss words. This is not a morphological relationship and cannot be done using SimpleNLG.

3.2 Language Model

We needed a language model to help choose the best word from a given set of translation gloss, and to decide when to add articles. The system first builds all words using the machine readable dictionary, and the morphological realizer outputting a list of sets, where each set contains the possible English words that the given Bliss word may translate to. The system looks at each set to determine if it contains nouns using wordnet (Miller, 1995). If a noun is found, then a set of articles *a, the,* or a blank is inserted before the set of nouns. From here, the language model needs to decide the most probable gloss words from each set, and also which article, if any, is most probable.

We created an N-gram model trained on the Gutenberg, brown, conll2000, and nps-chat corpora using NLTK (Bird and Loper, 2004). We used interpolation smoothing as in equation 1.

$$\begin{aligned} P(w_1, w_2, w_3) = c_1 P(w_3) + c_2 P(w_3|w_2) + ... \\ ... + C_n P(w_3|w_1, w_2) \\ s.t. \sum c_i = 1 c_1 < c_2 < c_n \end{aligned} \tag{1}$$

[3]www.github.com/usmansohail/Nighat

4 Test Set

We created a test set composed of 15 bliss utterances from children's books (Bruna, 1978; Andy and Mann, 1979; Chait, 1992; Cocking, 1979), 6 of which are shown in figure 6 for discussion.

5 Results

The translation system received a BLEU score of 34.53 when evaluated on the 15 utterance test set. Some sentences preserve the general meaning, whereas others do not. Some of the errors are related to the language model, while others are related to Blissymbolics. In Figure 6, examples 1, and 2 have errors that are related to the language model. Sentence 1 is missing an *a*. Sentence 3 is an example of a sentence that preserves the meaning, although it incorrectly translates *fat* to *thick*. The system translates *Julius* from sentence 2 and 1 to *a boy*. This translation relies on context to be interpreted correctly. Sentence 4 translates *other* to *you*. This error is caused by the fact that *you* and *other* are spelled the same way with a minor difference. The word *you* is spelled with *person* + 2, while *other* is spelled with *person [modified]* + 2. The current encoding scheme assigns each symbol with a unique ID, however modified symbols do not have a unique ID. Therefore, *person* and *person [modified]* both have the same ID. Figure 7 shows the difference between the two words.

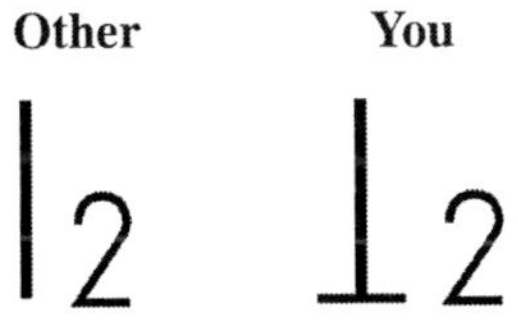

Figure 7: Other vs You

6 Future Work

In order to make a usable system, we think it is necessary to address the following topics:

1. **Encoding scheme**
   As the examples from figure 6 show, the current encoding scheme is not able to capture all of the capabilities of Bliss. In order to make a usable system, an encoding scheme needs to be chosen that can work with computer systems, and also preserves the capabilities of Bliss, such as modification of symbols.

2. **Language model**
   The language model that we used was implemented to show a proof of concept. In order to make the system more applicable, we think that the training corpora used should be composed primarily of dialogue utterances, since this is the way that the translation system is intended to be used.

3. **User Interface**
   If users are ever to use the system, there needs to exist a way for them to easily input. In order to build this, the encoding scheme needs to be chosen first. A critical component of a UI is a text to speech component so that users can be independent of a human interpreter.

4. **Context**
   A system that is able to exploit the context of a dialogue would decrease the reliance on a human interpreter. The way Bliss is used typically involves a human interpreter who can infer context, such as the name *Julius* from figure 6.

7 Conclusion

Our translation system adds some new features to Blissymbolics translation systems, namely the ability to create new words based on existing words. We also address some topics that need to be addressed for mainstream use. We believe our morphological perspective is useful for Blissymbolics, however more work is necessary to assess it's impact on translation. We hope to work with the Blissymbolics community for future work.

8 Acknowledgments

Special thanks to Anne O'Malley, Shirley McNaughton, Margareta Jennische, Annalu Waller, Lovisa Jacobson, and Blissymbolics Communication International.

	Reference Translation/Bliss	Result Translation
1	For Julius and his family 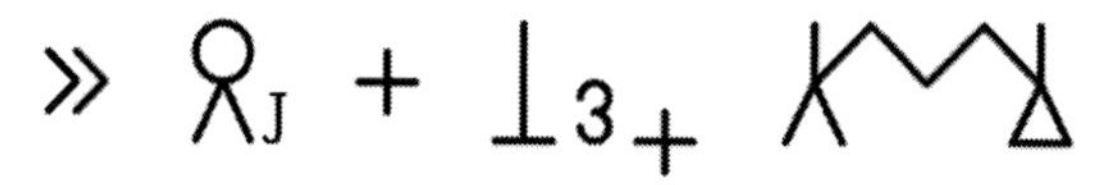	for **boy** and his family
2	Julius has many friends 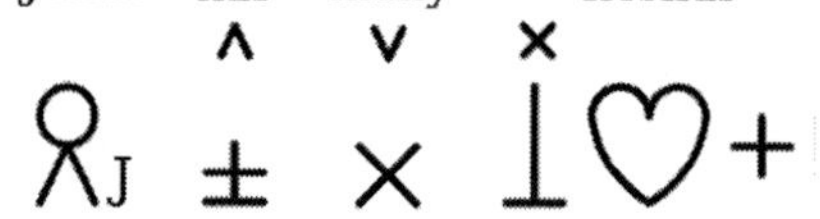	**a boy the gain much persons**
3	I have two fat fish 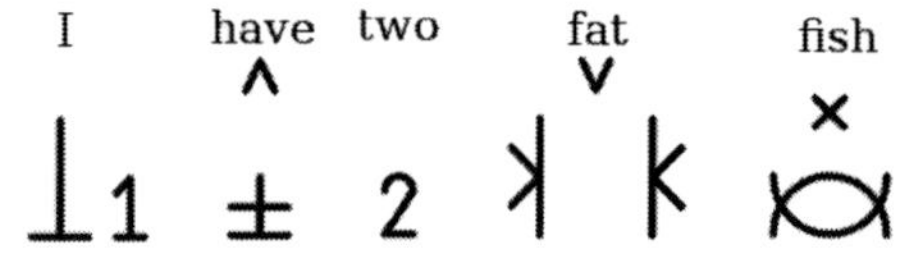	I have two **thick** fish
4	the other fat fish is called 	the **you the** fat fish is called bottom

Figure 6: Each row contains an utterance written in Bliss annotated with it's reference translation. Adjacent to that is the corresponding result translation using our system. Any written English inside of the Bliss utterance is taken as is.

References

Project gutenberg (n.d.). www.project.gutenberg.org. Accessed: 2018-7-29.

Andy and Gwen Mann. 1979. *Autumn*. University of Toronto Press.

Steven Bird and Edward Loper. 2004. Nltk: the natural language toolkit. In *Proceedings of the ACL 2004 on Interactive poster and demonstration sessions*, page 31. Association for Computational Linguistics.

Lindsey I Black, Anjel Vahratian, and Howard J Hoffman. 2015. Communication disorders and use of intervention services among children aged 3-17 years: United states, 2012. nchs data brief. number 205. *Centers for Disease Control and Prevention.*

Charles Kasiel Bliss. 1965. Semantography (blissymbolics): a simple system of 100 logical pictorial symbols, which can be operated and read like 1+ 2.

Dick Bruna. 1978. *I Can Dress Myself.* Methuen Publications.

Thelma Chait. 1992. *Julius and his friend the computer.* Oxford University Press Southern Africa.

Althea Cocking. 1979. *The Blissymbol Opposite Series: Book 1.*

Albert Gatt and Ehud Reiter. 2009. Simplenlg: A realisation engine for practical applications. In *Proceedings of the 12th European Workshop on Natural Language Generation*, pages 90–93. Association for Computational Linguistics.

George A Miller. 1995. Wordnet: a lexical database for english. *Communications of the ACM*, 38(11):39–41.

Paul Muter and Elizabeth E Johns. 1985. Learning logographies and alphabetic codes. *Human Learning*, 4:105–125.

Yael Netzer and Michael Elhadad. 2006. Using semantic authoring for blissymbols communication boards. In *Proceedings of the Human Language Technology Conference of the NAACL, Companion Volume: Short Papers*, NAACL-Short '06, pages 105–108, Stroudsburg, PA, USA. Association for Computational Linguistics.

Annalu Waller and Kris Jack. 2002. A predictive blissymbolic to english translation system. In *Proceedings of the fifth international ACM conference on Assistive technologies*, pages 186–191. ACM.

Investigating Speech Recognition for Improving Predictive AAC

Jiban Adhikary, Robbie Watling, Crystal Fletcher, Alex Stanage, Keith Vertanen
Michigan Technological University
Houghton, Michigan, USA
{jiban, rwatling, tafletch, amstanag, vertanen}@mtu.edu

Abstract

Making good letter or word predictions can help accelerate the communication of users of high-tech AAC devices. This is particularly important for real-time person-to-person conversations. We investigate whether performing speech recognition on the speaking-side of a conversation can improve language model based predictions. We compare the accuracy of three plausible microphone deployment options and the accuracy of two commercial speech recognition engines (Google and IBM Watson). We found that despite recognition word error rates of 7–16%, our ensemble of N-gram and recurrent neural network language models made predictions nearly as good as when they used the reference transcripts.

1 Introduction

People who are non-verbal often use some form of Augmentative and Alternative Communication (AAC). Common forms of speaking disorders include stuttering, cluttering, apraxia, dysarthria, aphasia, Parkinson's disease, amyotrophic lateral sclerosis (ALS), or cerebral palsy. An AAC device may let a user select letters, words, and phrases from its interface and a communication partner can read the text or hear it via text-to-speech. The rate at which an AAC user can enter text is typically slow (often less than 10 words-per-minute) (Trnka et al., 2009; Simpson et al., 2006; Higginbotham et al., 2007). That is why predictive AAC devices normally use a language model to try and make suggestions of likely upcoming text. These predictions are usually made based solely on the text entered by the AAC user. They typically ignore the two-way nature of conversation which can offer many contextual clues.

In this paper, first we investigate how to record and recognize the speech of a partner communicating with the AAC user. Then we investigate if speech recognition on partner speech improves two-sided conversational language modeling.

2 Related Work

Predictive AAC devices typically use an N-gram language model (LM). An N-gram LM calculates the probability of a token given the previous N-1 tokens. The performance of this model depends on the training data being closely matched to a user's text. But for practical, ethical, and privacy issues, there is a scarcity of text written by AAC users. Researchers have resorted to training LMs on data from news articles (Trnka et al., 2009) or phone transcripts (Wandmacher et al., 2008). Another option is the large amounts of text that can be mined from the internet, e.g. tweets, blog posts, or Wikipedia articles. While such web data may be informal or have other artifacts such as abbreviations, researchers have used filtering methods such as cross entropy difference selection (Moore and Lewis, 2010) to select training data for AAC language models (Vertanen and Kristensson, 2011).

Recently, recurrent neural network language models (RNNLMs) have achieved state-of-the-art performance over traditional N-gram language models. RNNLMs have been shown to better model long range dependencies when combined with techniques such as long short-term memory (Hochreiter and Schmidhuber, 1997) or gated units (Chung et al., 2014). Further gains have also been achieved by interpolating N-gram models (Mikolov et al., 2014) and other techniques (Mikolov et al., 2011a,b).

In addition to using textual context, previous AAC work has also investigated using face detection (Kane et al., 2012), vision (Kane and Morris, 2017), and location (Demmans Epp et al., 2012) as context for AAC predictions. But limited work has been done to predict AAC user's response based on partner speech. Wisenburn (2008; 2009) created a program called Converser and used speech recognition to identify the speaking partner's words. This input was then parsed by a

Proceedings of the Eighth Workshop on Speech and Language Processing for Assistive Technologies, pages 37–43
Minneapolis, Minnesota, USA ©2019 Association for Computational Linguistics

A:	Did you call the theater?
B:	So sorry, I forgot to call the theater.
A:	You can just go online.
B:	That's true, I'll do that now.
A:	What movie is it that you want to see?
B:	The lord of the rings.

Table 1: A dialogue created by Amazon Turk workers.

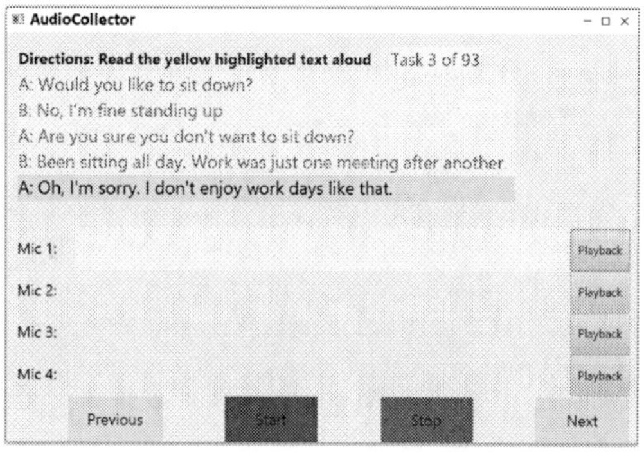

Figure 1: The application used to record dialogues.

noun phrase identification system. Identified noun phrases, along with relevant static messages, were displayed to the user. This provided users with a faster communication rate compared to a system that did not use partner speech. In our work, we also perform speech recognition on the partner's speech. However, we will use recognition results as context to our language models in hopes of better predicting an AAC user's upcoming text.

3 Speech Data Collection

Our first step was to obtain text and audio data reasonably representative of everyday person-to-person conversations. In this section, we detail how we collected this data. Further, we designed our collection to answer the practical question of how and where a microphone might be located for recording a partner's speech.

As a starting point for our spoken dialogue collection, we used the text dialogues collected by Vertanen (2017). These dialogues were invented by workers on Amazon Mechanical Turk. The dialogue started with a question invented by one of the workers. Subsequent workers then extended the dialogue by another turn until a total of six turns were completed. Table 1 shows an example dialogue. The original collection had 1,419 dialogues. We removed 265 we deemed potentially offensive, resulting in a set of 1,154 dialogues.

3.1 Audio Data Collection

The dialogue data from (Vertanen, 2017) consisted only of text. We wanted to investigate whether a partner's speech could improve an AAC device's predictions. We designed a desktop application to record audio data of participants' speaking turns in the text dialogues. The application highlighted the current turn we wanted the participant to speak. Any previous turns of the dialogue were also shown as context. The application recorded from three microphones simultaneously:

- HEADSET — A Logitech H390 USB noise cancelling headset microphone.
- LAPTOP — The built-in microphone of a 13" 2015 MacBook Pro laptop.
- CONFERENCE — A MXL AC404 USB conference microphone. This microphone was positioned behind the laptop at a distance of approximately 0.9 m from the participant.

The application allowed the participant to re-record any utterances in which they misspoke. We analyzed just the last recording for each dialogue turn. Audio was recorded at 44.1 kHz. We recruited 14 participants via convenience sampling. Four self-reported as male, ten as female. The average age was 36. Participant 5 reported having a foreign accent. Each participant took part in an approximately half-hour session and was paid $10. Participants sat at a desk with a laptop in quiet office. They were allowed to adjust their chair so they could comfortably operate the laptop.

Participants first recorded three practice dialogues. We did not analyze the practice dialogues. Each participant then completed half the turns in 28 additional dialogues. The subsequent participant completed the other half of the turns of the same 28 dialogues. In total, we collected 1,176 utterances constituting both sides of 196 dialogues. We have made our filtered text dialogues, audio recordings, recognition results, and Java audio collection application available to other researchers[1].

3.2 Speech Recognition Experiments

We performed speech recognition using two commercially available speech recognizers, Google Cloud Speech-to-Text and IBM Watson Speech-to-Text. We performed speech recognition on audio from each of the three different microphones.

[1]`https://digitalcommons.mtu.edu/data-files/1`

		Microphone	
	LAPTOP	HEADSET	CONF.
GOOGLE	7.3±1.0	7.0±1.0	8.9±1.2
WATSON	10.5± 1.2	10.7±1.2	16.0±1.6

Table 2: Word Error Rate (WER %) using different microphones and speech recognizers. Results are formatted as mean ± 95% bootstrap confidence intervals.

We computed the Word Error Rate (WER) of each recognition result against its reference transcript.

The reference transcripts included various numeric characters representing times or amounts. We found the recognition results on such turns were variable. Sometimes the recognizer returned numeric transcriptions and sometimes numbers were spelled out as words. For consistency, we dropped all dialogues if any of its reference turns had a number in it. This reduced the number of dialogues from 196 to 160.

As shown in Table 2, the mean WER on the three different microphones using the GOOGLE recognizer was LAPTOP 7.3%, HEADSET 7.0%, and CONFERENCE 8.9%. IBM's recognizer had higher error rates with LAPTOP at 10.5%, HEADSET at 10.7%, and CONFERENCE at 16.0%.

Figure 2 shows the WER for each participant using the GOOGLE speech recognizer and audio from the HEADSET microphone. 9 of the 14 participants had a lower mean WER of 5.5%. This was driven by the fact that 84.0% of their utterance turns were recognized with no errors.

We recorded our audio in a quiet office. We also wanted to explore how our methods might work in noisier locations. To do this, we injected a recording of street noise into our clean audio data. We used the SoX Sound eXchange utility to add in the street noise at three different volume levels: 0.1, 0.2, and 0.3. Figure 3 shows the mean word error rates on recordings with no noise and at the three noise levels. Even at noise volume level 0.3, both recognizers' mean word error rates using the HEADSET and LAPTOP microphones stayed below 40%. However, the mean word error rates using the CONFERENCE microphone started deteriorating more sharply with increasing noise.

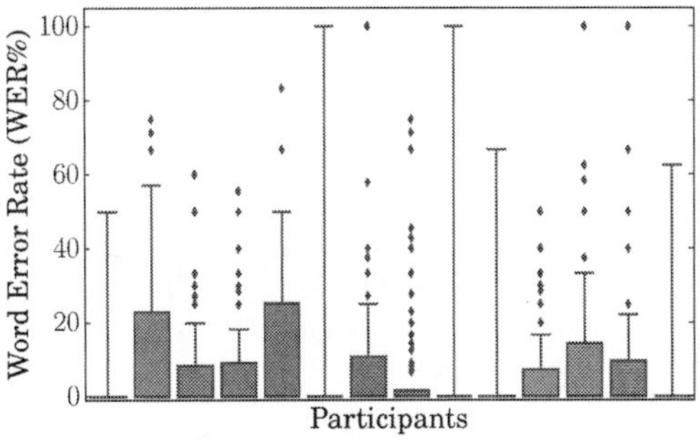

Figure 2: Participants' per utterance WER using the Google recognizer and audio from a headset mic.

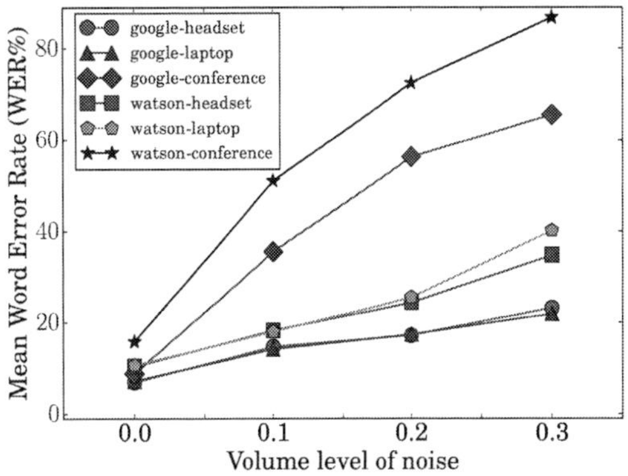

Figure 3: WER on audio dialogue turns without noise and with three different injected noise levels.

4 Language Modeling Experiments

We now investigate how to use language models to better predict turns in our dialogue collection. Recall we recorded both sides of 196 of the dialogues from our set of 1,154 dialogues. After dropping dialogues with numbers, we arrived at a test set of 160 dialogues with audio data. We created text-only training and development sets from the remaining 958 dialogues. From these dialogues, we dropped 128 that contained numbers. We randomly selected 160 from the remaining dialogues as a development set and 670 as a training set.

Our language modeling experiments used a vocabulary of 35 K words. The vocabulary consisted of the most frequent known English words occurring in 50 M words of sentences parsed from Twitter. Any words not in this vocabulary were mapped to an unknown word token. We converted text to lowercase and removed punctuation aside from apostrophe. Throughout, we report the per-word perplexity of our test set (160 dialogues, 960 turns, 7.1 K words). We excluded the sentence end pseudo-word from our calculations.

4.1 N-gram Language Models

We took each turn in the training set as an independent training example (4,020 turns, 30 K words). We trained a 4-gram interpolated modified Kneser-Ney model using SRILM (Stolcke, 2002;

Training data	Words	PPL
Twitter, small amount of data	30 K	417.3
Crowd dialogues	30 K	211.8
Twitter, large amount of data	50 M	96.0
+ CE diff. 25% dialogues	50 M	91.0
+ CE diff. 50% dialogues	50 M	86.8
+ CE diff. 75% dialogues	50 M	83.5
+ CE diff. 100% dialogues	50 M	83.5
+ Optimized CE threshold	50 M	77.4

Table 3: N-gram perplexity varying training data.

Stolcke et al., 2011). As shown in Table 3, the perplexity on the test set was 211.8. For comparison, we trained a 4-gram model on 30 K words of random Twitter data collected via Twitter's streaming API between 2009–2015. The Twitter model had a much higher perplexity of 417.3.

An approach to filtering an out-of-domain training data is cross-entropy difference selection (Moore and Lewis, 2010). This approach calculates the cross-entropy of individual sentences under an in-domain and an out-of-domain model trained on similar amounts of data. We trained our in-domain model on between 25–100% of the text in our Turk dialogue training set.

We selected 50 M words of Twitter data below a certain cross-entropy difference threshold. We used an initial threshold of -0.3. The more negative the threshold, the more sentences had to resemble in-domain text in order to be selected. As shown in Table 3, using more in-domain data reduced perplexity though gains eventually flattened. Finally, we used all the in-domain data to search for the optimal cross-entropy difference threshold on the development set. The optimal threshold of -0.06 further lowered perplexity to 77.

4.2 RNN Language Models

Next, we investigated training Recurrent Neural Network Language Models (RNNLMs) on the cross-entropy difference selected Twitter data. We trained our models using the Faster RNNLM toolkit[2]. For each model type, we trained 10 RNNLMs with different random initialization seeds. We report the perplexity on the test set of the model that had the lowest perplexity on the development set. Unless otherwise noted, we used the default hyperparameters of Faster RNNLM.

[2] https://github.com/yandex/faster-rnnlm

Model	PPL Sentence	PPL Dialogue
Twitter RNNLM	179.0	129.3
+ GRUs	167.8	122.8
+ NCE	172.2	111.9
+ maximum entropy	123.7	84.1
+ Twitter 4-gram LM	75.2	71.5
+ unigram cache	75.2	68.5

Table 4: Perplexities with added features. We reset the RNNLM between each sentence or after each dialogue.

During evaluation we reinitialized the RNNLM after every sentence or after every six-turn dialogue. This allowed us to observe how much the model was adapting to a particular dialogue while avoiding allowing the model to adapt to the general style of our Turk dialogues.

As shown in Table 4, a model trained with 250 sigmoid units had a perplexity of 129.3 on each dialogue. Switching to 250 Gated Recurrent Units (GRUs) (Chung et al., 2014) reduced perplexity to 122.8. Switching to Noise Contrastive Estimation (NCE) (Chen et al., 2015) further reduced perplexity to 111.9. Training a maximum entropy language model of size 1000 and order 4 in the RNN reduced perplexity substantially to 84.1.

We interpolated our best RNNLM with our best previous N-gram model. We optimized the mixture weights with respect to our development set. This further reduced perplexity to 71.5. We also investigated a unigram cache (Grave et al., 2016). Similar to the RNNLM, we reset the cache after each sentence or after each dialogue. The cache model provided a small reduction in perplexity to 68.5. The mixture weights were: N-gram 0.55, RNNLM 0.42, and unigram cache 0.04.

Comparing the result columns in Table 4, we see consistently higher perplexities when the RNNLM was evaluated on sentences instead of on entire dialogues. In particular, the RNNLM was substantially worse with a perplexity of 123.7 on sentences versus 84.1 on dialogues. This demonstrates the ability of the RNNLM to adapt to aspects of the text over a longer time horizon.

4.3 Two-sided Dialogue Language Models

We now turn to training language models on two-sided dialogues. Since our Amazon Turk dialogue collection is relatively small, we instead used dialogues from movies (Danescu-Niculescu-Mizil and Lee, 2011). We created a training set

Model	PPL
Movie dialogue 7-gram	138.5
Movie dialogue RNNLM	129.1
Turk dialogue RNNLM	185.5
Mixture, dialogue models	104.3
Mixture, Twitter + dialogue + cache	66.3

Table 5: Perplexity of models trained on two-sided dialogues and mixtures of dialogue and twitter models.

of 83 K dialogues consisting of 305 K turns and 3.2 M words. We introduced a pseudo-word to denote speaker changes. We excluded this speaker change word from our perplexity calculations. We treated the set of turns making up a dialogue as a single "sentence" during training and testing. We evaluated models on each dialogue in our Turk test set (the same set used previously). In the case of RNNLMs, we reset the model after each dialogue.

We first tested 4-gram through 8-gram N-gram models. The 4-gram had the highest perplexity of 139.2 The 7-gram model had the best perplexity of 138.5 (Table 5). Next we trained a RNNLM on the movie dialogues using 300 GRU units, NCE, and with a maximum entropy model of size 1000, order 4. The RNNLM had a lower perplexity of 129.1. This again highlights the ability of the RNNLM to better model long-range dependencies and/or topics compared to the N-gram model.

We also trained an RNNLM on just the Turk dialogues. We used 100 GRU units, NCE, and a maximum entropy model with 100 units and an order of 4. This model had a perplexity of 185.5. We think this model's worse performance reflects the substantially smaller amount of training data. By interpolating these three dialogue models, we obtained an even lower perplexity of 104.3. The mixture weights were: Movie 7-gram 0.24, Movie RNNLM 0.40, and Turk RNNLM 0.37.

Our two-sided models were trained on modest amounts of data. To see if they still offered gains in combination with models trained on substantially more Twitter data, we interpolated all our models. The mixture weights were: Twitter N-gram 0.43, Twitter RNNLM 0.32, movie dialogue N-gram 0.05, movie dialogue RNNLM 0.10, Turk dialogue RNNLM 0.06, and unigram cache 0.04. The mixture model's perplexity was 66.3, a modest gain compared to the 68.5 obtained using a mixture of the Twitter models and unigram cache. It does however represent a more substantial gain compared to the 77.4 of the best N-gram only model. This shows that having access to both sides of a dialogue combined with the adaptive nature of RNNLMs may offer improved predictive AAC.

4.4 Impact of Speech Recognition Errors

In real-time person-to-person conversations, we cannot expect to have a perfect transcript of the other side of the conversation. We now investigate the impact of speech recognition errors on the performance of our language models. We did this by measuring the perplexity on two copies of the test set. In the first copy, we replaced the transcript of the even number dialogue turns with the speech recognition result of one of our participants speaking that turn. In the second copy, we replaced the odd number turns. We report the perplexity calculated from the odd turns from the first copy and the even turns from the second copy.

The entire six turns were provided to the language models for both copies to allow the model to condition on prior turns (including any speech errors). We reset the RNNLMs and unigram cache model between each dialogue. We used the previous best ensemble of six models which had a perplexity on the test dialogues of 66.3. We tested injecting the speech recognition results from the three microphones, two recognition engines, and four noise levels (none, 0.1, 0.2, and 0.3).

As shown in Figure 4, the perplexity of our ensemble of models only increased slightly when we replaced the reference transcripts with speech recognition results based on noise-free audio. For example, the far-field conference microphone had a WER of 8.9%. However, the errors introduced by recognition only slightly increased the perplexity of the dialogues from 66.3 to 66.6. Similar to WER in Figure 3, as the level of injected noise increased, perplexities also increased.

5 Discussion and Limitations

In this paper, we conducted an initial investigation into the feasibility of performing speech recognition on an AAC user's speaking partner. We found that whether audio was captured from a wired headset or from a far-field microphone, we could recognize conversational-style utterances with error rates between 7–16%. We found Google's speech engine provided more accurate recognition than the IBM Watson recognizer. However, IBM's engine offers other benefits such as exposing probabilistic information about recognition re-

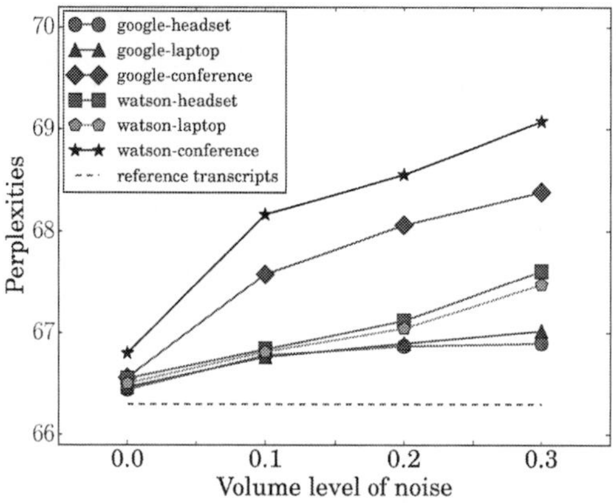

Figure 4: Perplexities using speech recognition on partner turns rather than reference transcripts. Results for no added noise, and for three levels of injected noise.

sults (e.g. a word confusion network). Such information might be leveraged to help avoid conditioning a predictive AAC interface on erroneous regions of a partner's speech recognition result.

Our participants were given the verbatim text for each of their dialogue turns. As such, we can expect they spoke more fluently than one could expect in a spontaneous conversation. Further, we only collected audio in a quiet environment. While our results seem robust to artificially added noise, it remains to be seen if this holds for real-world noisy environments. As such, our error rates probably represent a lower-bound of what could be expected. Nonetheless, it is reassuring that our language models predict the non-speaking side's text with only minimal perplexity loses despite relying on text obtained via speech recognition.

Thus far we have focused on ascertaining whether there is a potential advantage to conditioning on recognition of the speaking side. Whether the perplexity gains we showed will result in actual practical improvements in the auspices of a predictive AAC interface remain to be seen. Further work is needed to understand whether these language model gains will result in, for example, better word predictions that actually save a user keystrokes. Even more work is needed to validate if end-user performance improves.

The use of speech recognition by an AAC device also has obvious privacy implications. This may require the AAC device or user to allow partners to opt-in to having their voice recognized. Further, our current work used cloud-based speech recognition. Users may prefer to have their speech recognized locally on device. Local recognition may also be necessary to avoid network latency or to allow use without network connectivity.

Our goal here was to demonstrate some of the building blocks necessary for modeling everyday conversational-style text. While we made some effort to optimize our models (e.g. tuning mixture weights on development data), further improvements are certainly possible. For example, we did not conduct an extensive search for the best hyperparameters used during RNNLM training. Further, we need to investigate whether our methods and results scale to substantially more training data.

Our results show the benefits of language models based on recurrent neural networks. In particular, we found even when trained on non-dialogue data, RNNLMs adapted to the content of our short dialogues, providing good gains compared to an N-gram model. Further, we showed how a small in-domain corpus can be used to optimize models for everyday conversations. Despite our relatively small amount of two-sided dialogues data (3.2 M words of movie dialogues), we obtained improvements compared to using models trained only on much more non-dialogue data (50 M words of Twitter). In the end, we found an ensemble of N-gram and RNNLMs trained on sentence and dialogues combined with a unigram cache model provided the best performance.

6 Conclusions

AAC users often face challenges in taking part in everyday conversations due to their typically slow text entry rates. Predictions can provide an opportunity to accelerate their communication rate, but it is crucial these predictions be as accurate as possible. Leveraging real-world contextual clues offers one route to improving these predictions. In this paper, we found speech can be accurately recognized with a variety of microphone configurations that might be deployed on an AAC device. Further, we found the error rates of current state-of-the-art recognizers allowed predictions nearly as good as having the verbatim text of the partner's turn. We think this work provides promising results showing a partner's speech can provide context to improve an AAC device's predictions.

7 Acknowledgements

This material is based upon work supported by the NSF under Grant No. IIS-1750193.

References

Xie Chen, Xunying Liu, Mark J.F. Gales, and Philip C. Woodland. 2015. Recurrent neural network language model training with noise contrastive estimation for speech recognition. In *IEEE International Conference on Acoustics, Speech and Signal Processing*, ICASSP '15, pages 5411–5415.

Junyoung Chung, Caglar Gulcehre, KyungHyun Cho, and Yoshua Bengio. 2014. Empirical evaluation of gated recurrent neural networks on sequence modeling. *arXiv preprint arXiv:1412.3555*.

Cristian Danescu-Niculescu-Mizil and Lillian Lee. 2011. Chameleons in imagined conversations: A new approach to understanding coordination of linguistic style in dialogs. In *Proceedings of the 2nd Workshop on Cognitive Modeling and Computational Linguistics*, pages 76–87. Association for Computational Linguistics.

Carrie Demmans Epp, Justin Djordjevic, Shimu Wu, Karyn Moffatt, and Ronald M Baecker. 2012. Towards providing just-in-time vocabulary support for assistive and augmentative communication. In *Proceedings of the 2012 ACM international conference on Intelligent User Interfaces*, pages 33–36. ACM.

Edouard Grave, Armand Joulin, and Nicolas Usunier. 2016. Improving neural language models with a continuous cache. *arXiv preprint arXiv:1612.04426*.

D. Jeffery Higginbotham, Howard Shane, Susanne Russell, and Kevin Caves. 2007. Access to AAC: Present, past, and future. *Augmentative and Alternative Communication*, 23(3):243–257.

Sepp Hochreiter and Jürgen Schmidhuber. 1997. Long short-term memory. *Neural computation*, 9(8):1735–1780.

Shaun K Kane, Barbara Linam-Church, Kyle Althoff, and Denise McCall. 2012. What we talk about: designing a context-aware communication tool for people with aphasia. In *Proceedings of the 14th international ACM SIGACCESS conference on Computers and accessibility*, pages 49–56. ACM.

Shaun K Kane and Meredith Ringel Morris. 2017. Let's talk about x: Combining image recognition and eye gaze to support conversation for people with ALS. In *Proceedings of the 2017 Conference on Designing Interactive Systems*, pages 129–134. ACM.

Tomáš Mikolov, Anoop Deoras, Stefan Kombrink, Lukas Burget, and Jan Cernockỳ. 2011a. Empirical evaluation and combination of advanced language modeling techniques. In *Proceedings of the International Conference on Spoken Language Processing*, pages 605–608.

Tomáš Mikolov, Armand Joulin, Sumit Chopra, Michael Mathieu, and Marc'Aurelio Ranzato. 2014. Learning longer memory in recurrent neural networks. *arXiv preprint arXiv:1412.7753*.

Tomáš Mikolov, Stefan Kombrink, Lukáš Burget, Jan Černockỳ, and Sanjeev Khudanpur. 2011b. Extensions of recurrent neural network language model. In *IEEE International Conference on Acoustics, Speech and Signal Processing*, ICASSP '11, pages 5528–5531.

Robert C. Moore and William Lewis. 2010. Intelligent selection of language model training data. In *Proceedings of the ACL 2010 Conference Short Papers*, ACLShort '10, pages 220–224, Stroudsburg, PA, USA. Association for Computational Linguistics.

Richard Simpson, Heidi Koester, and Ed LoPresti. 2006. Evaluation of an adaptive row/column scanning system. *Technology and disability*, 18(3):127–138.

Andreas Stolcke. 2002. SRILM – an extensible language modeling toolkit. In *Seventh International Conference on Spoken Language Processing*, pages 901–904, Denver, CO.

Andreas Stolcke, Jing Zheng, Wen Wang, and Victor Abrash. 2011. SRILM at sixteen: Update and outlook. In *Proceedings of IEEE Automatic Speech Recognition and Understanding Workshop*, volume 5 of *ASRU '11*.

Keith Trnka, John McCaw, Debra Yarrington, Kathleen F McCoy, and Christopher Pennington. 2009. User interaction with word prediction: The effects of prediction quality. *ACM Transactions on Accessible Computing (TACCESS)*, 1(3):17.

Keith Vertanen. 2017. Towards improving predictive aac using crowdsourced dialogues and partner context. In *ASSETS '17: Proceedings of the ACM SIGACCESS Conference on Computers and Accessibility (poster)*, pages 347–348.

Keith Vertanen and Per Ola Kristensson. 2011. The imagination of crowds: Conversational AAC language modeling using crowdsourcing and large data sources. In *Proceedings of the Conference on Empirical Methods in Natural Language Processing*, EMNLP'11, pages 700–711. Association for Computational Linguistics.

Tonio Wandmacher, Jean-Yves Antoine, Franck Poirier, and Jean-Paul Départe. 2008. Sibylle, an assistive communication system adapting to the context and its user. *ACM Transactions on Accessible Computing (TACCESS)*, 1(1):6.

Bruce Wisenburn and D. Jeffery Higginbotham. 2008. An AAC application using speaking partner speech recognition to automatically produce contextually relevant utterances: objective results. *Augmentative and Alternative Communication*, 24(2):100–109.

Bruce Wisenburn and D. Jeffery Higginbotham. 2009. Participant evaluations of rate and communication efficacy of an AAC application using natural language processing. *Augmentative and Alternative Communication*, 25(2):78–89.

Noisy Neural Language Modeling for Typing Prediction in BCI Communication

Rui Dong **David A. Smith**
Khoury College of Computer Sciences
Northeastern University
Boston, MA
{dongrui, dasmith}@ccs.neu.edu

Shiran Dudy **Steven Bedrick**
Center for Spoken Language Understanding
Oregon Health & Science University
Portland, OR
{dudy,bedricks}@ohsu.edu

Abstract

Language models have broad adoption in predictive typing tasks. When the typing history contains numerous errors, as in open-vocabulary predictive typing with brain-computer interface (BCI) systems, we observe significant performance degradation in both n-gram and recurrent neural network language models trained on clean text. In evaluations of ranking character predictions, training recurrent LMs on noisy text makes them much more robust to noisy histories, even when the error model is misspecified. We also propose an effective strategy for combining evidence from multiple ambiguous histories of BCI electroencephalogram measurements.

1 Introduction

Brain-computer interface (BCI) systems provide a means of language communication for people who have lost the ability to speak, write, or type, e.g., patients with amyotrophic lateral sclerosis (ALS) or locked-in syndrome (LIS). These systems are designed to detect a user's intent from electroencephalogram (EEG) or other signals and to translate them into typing commands.

Recent studies have shown that incorporating language information into BCI systems can significantly improve both their typing speed and accuracy (Oken et al., 2014; Mora-Cortes et al., 2014; Speier et al., 2016, 2017, 2018; Dudy et al., 2018). Existing methods for optimizing BCI systems with language information either focus on improving the accuracy of symbol classifiers by adding priors from language models(Oken et al., 2014), or on accelerating the typing speed by tying prediction (Dudy et al., 2018), word completion, or automatic error correction (Ghosh and Kristensson, 2017).

Instead of displaying a keyboard layout, these BCI systems present candidate characters sequentially, as in the Shannon game (Shannon, 1951), and then measure users' reactions with EEG or other signals. Predictive performance is thus measured using the mean reciprocal rank of the correct character or the recall of the correct character in the k candidates presented in a batch to the user.

Most previous work on language modeling for BCI employs n-gram language models although the past decade has seen recurrent and other neural architectures surpass these models for many tasks. Furthermore, most predictive typing methods, for BCI or other applications, depend on language models trained on clean text; however, BCI output often contains noise due to misclassification of EEG or other input signals. To the best of our knowledge, language models have rarely been evaluated in with such character-level noise. Recurrent language models, however, could effectively utilize contexts of 200 tokens on average (Khandelwal et al., 2018). Although this might be a disadvantage with noisy histories, we will see that it is no worse than n-gram models with clean training and much better with noisy training.

In addition, existing work mainly focuses on prediction given a single sequence of tokens in the history, but the signal classifier for BCI systems might not always correctly rank the users' intent as the top candidate. Dudy et al. (2018) proposed incorporating ambiguous history into decoding with a joint word-character finite-state model, but typing prediction could not be further improved. Although (Sperber et al., 2017) considered lattice decoding for neural models, the task of integrating multiple candidate histories during online prediction has not been studied.

To address these challenges, we propose to train a noise-tolerant neural language model for online predictive typing and to provide a richer understanding of the effect of the noise on recurrent neural network language models. We aim to an-

Proceedings of the Eighth Workshop on Speech and Language Processing for Assistive Technologies, pages 44–51
Minneapolis, Minnesota, USA

swer the following questions: (1) what effect noise in different regions of the history and in different sentence and word positions has on recurrent language model character predictions; (2) how to mitigate performance degradation in LM predictive accuracy with noisy histories; and (3) whether including ambiguous history could help to improve the performance of neural language models.

In this paper, we investigate these questions by training long short-term memory (LSTM: Hochreiter and Schmidhuber, 1997) models on synthetic noisy data generated from the New York Times (NYT) corpus and the SUBTLEXus corpus to cover both formal and colloquial language.

Experimental results show that injecting noise into the training data improves the generalizability of language models on a predictive typing task. Moreover, a neural language model trained on noisy text outperforms n-gram language models trained on noisy or clean text. In fact, some language models trained on clean text do substantially worse than a character unigram baseline when presented with text with only uniform stationary noise. Taking multiple possible candidates into consideration at each time step further improves predictive performance.

2 Related Work

Language Modeling for BCI Systems As noted above, several BCI systems have incorporated n-gram language models trained on clean text (Oken et al., 2014; Speier et al., 2016, 2017). Dudy et al. (2018) propose taking noisy ambiguous outputs from BCI signal classifiers and using a language model to find an optimal path among those output to predict the next letter. Their use of ambiguous histories, however, does not significantly improve performance for a word-character hybrid model.

Noisy Language Models Xie et al. (2017) show that injecting noise into training data for neural network grammar-correction models could achieve comparable performance with parameter regularization and thus make the model more generalizable with limited training data. Belinkov and Bisk (2017) show that machine translation models trained on noisy source text are more robust to the corresponding type of noise. Li et al. (2013) aim at using fixed-history neural network models to analyze the typing stream and predict the next character. Ghosh and Kristensson (2017) describe training a sequence-to-sequence model with attention to automatically correct and complete the current context. Their word-level decoder cannot predict unseen words, as a character or word-character hybrid model could naturally do.

3 Approach

Given an input sequence of characters typed by a user, the goal of typing prediction is to predict the next possible character that the user intends to type, which is the usual objective of language modeling. Both typing speed and typing accuracy could be significantly increased if the user's intended character is ranked higher and presented earlier to the user at each time step. We apply LSTM model, which has been proven effective in capturing long-term dependencies, as our language model.

In this paper, we aim to study the effects of noise in the input sequence on the performance of language models for typing prediction in BCI systems. As shown by Belinkov and Bisk (2017) and Xie et al. (2017), the performance of language models and translation models degrades dramatically on text unobserved in the training corpus, but adding appropriate noise to the training corpus could significantly improve accuracy. We therefore propose to generate synthetic noisy data by randomly choosing p percent of characters from both the training and test corpus, and substituting for them a random character excluding the original correct one. Here we use uniform distribution to sample the characters. We then train the language models on the corrupted training set and compare their performance on the corrupted test set.

4 Experiments

In this section, we first introduce the details of our experimental setup (§4.1). Then we compare the performance of the LSTM and baseline models trained on clean and noisy text (§4.2). Further discussion of the effect of errors on LSTM models follows in §4.3 and §4.4. §4.5 explores whether including multiple candidate histories could further improve predictive performance.

4.1 Experimental Setup

Datasets We evaluate our model on two datasets: the New York Times (NTY) corpus (Sandhaus, 2008) and SUBTLEXus (Brysbaert and New,

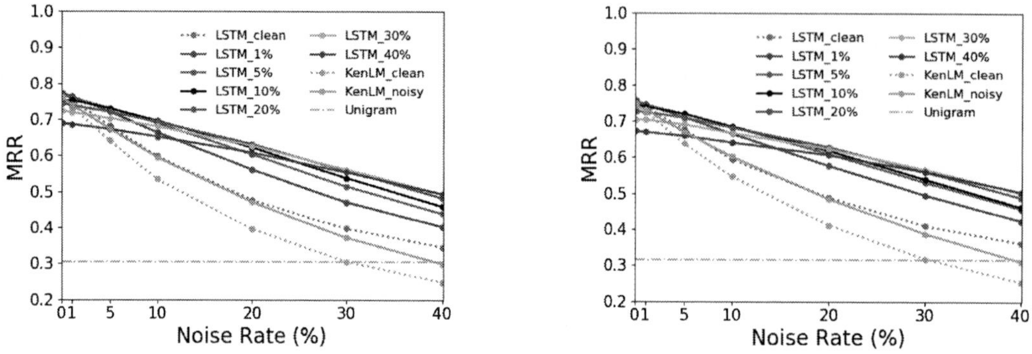

(a) NYT (b) SUBTLEXus

Figure 1: MRR of different models for predictive typing on test sets with different noise rates

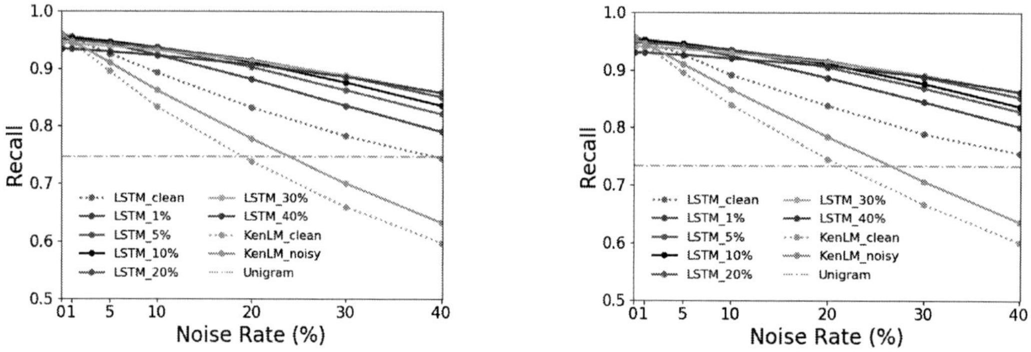

(a) NYT (b) SUBTLEXus

Figure 2: Recall of different models for predictive typing on test sets with different noise rates

2009) corpus of subtitles from movies and television. The NYT has relatively longer sentences, richer vocabulary, and more formal language; SUBTLEXus tends toward colloquial language and shorter sentences. To make a fair comparison between the two corpora, we randomly sample two subsets from them with equal numbers of characters. Both corpora are split into sentences, 80% sentences are randomly sampled as training set while the rest are used as test set. Table 1 summarizes the data.

Dataset	# Sentences	Avg length	Std of Length
NYT	1,750,000	120.11	64.78
SUBTLEXus	5,602,082	37.54	33.42

Table 1: Corpus sentence count and average character length

Baselines and Comparison We compare the LSTM model with two baselines: a character unigram language model (Unigram) and a character n-gram language model with Kneser-Ney smoothing trained with KenLM (Heafield, 2011). Here we set n as 9 and filter all the n-grams appearing less than 5 times. We also compare the LSTM with the OCLM model (Dudy et al., 2018), a joint word-character finite-state model, on the predictive typing task with a ambiguous history. Our LSTM model has 3 layers with 512 hidden units for each layer.

Evaluation Metrics Mean reciprocal rank at 10 (MRR@10) and Recall at 10 (Recall@10) are used for evaluation. Recall@10 reflects whether the correct characters are included in the top 10 candidates suggested by a language model; MRR@10 reveals the rank of the correct character. We use MRR and Recall for short in the following sections. The average values of each metric across all time steps of all sequences are reported.

4.2 Main Results

In this experiment, we compare the LSTM models with Unigram and KenLM models on predictive typing. We first train all the models on clean text to get LSTM_clean, KenLM_clean and Unigram. LSTM and KenLM models are then trained on text with p percent of noise to get the noisy models {LSTM,KenLM}_$p\%$ ($p \in \{1, 5, 10, 20, 30, 40\}$). Since the focus of this paper is on noisy LSTM models, we summarize the performance of all noisy KenLM models as KenLM_noisy: for a given test set, we run KenLM_$p\%$ for each p in $\{1, 5, 10, 20, 30, 40\}$ and choose the best performance as the performance of KenLM_noisy. Then we compare these models on test sets with noise rates varying from 0% (clean) to 40%. Figures 1 and 2 present the performance of all the language models trained on clean or noisy text when evaluating on noisy text.

Noisy or Clean Model? We see that both noisy LSTM models and KenLM models significantly outperform their corresponding clean models on noisy test sets. Although LSTM_clean and KenLM_clean achieve the best performance on clean test data, their performance drops dramatically when applied to noisy data. At 30% noise, KenLM is no better than a unigram baseline; LSTM_clean does not suffer quite as much. The language models trained on clean text are sensitive to the noise rate of the test data, while the language models trained on noisy data performs more robustly, even when only 1% noise is added. Therefore, injecting noise into the training corpus could significantly improve the generalizability of language models on unseen noisy data.

Neural or N-gram Language Model? Figures 1 and 2 show that the accuracy of LSTM models is more stable on unseen noisy text than n-gram models. This advantage, we conjecture, results not only from the LSTMs' incorporation of longer contexts (which might be a disadvantage, but see below), but also because the parameter counts of n-gram models rise with the amount of noise. Even LSTM_clean achieves much higher Recall than KenLM_noisy on test sets with different noise rates. The gap in Recall between them becomes larger when the data is much noisier; however, the difference between their MRR is not that significant. This indicates that errors in the typing history have a more significant impact on the MRR than the Recall of the LSTM_clean model.

How to Choose the Training Noise Rate? The performance of LSTM models trained with different noise rates reveals that all the noisy models works worse on noisier data. But a model performs better when trained and tested on data with matching noise rates. It is unsurprising that LSTM_40% works worst on the test data with 1% of noise, while LSTM_1% works worst on the test set with 40% of noise. When the noise rate of the test set is unknown, training the model with only 10% percent of noise is acceptable for test data with noise rates less than 40%.

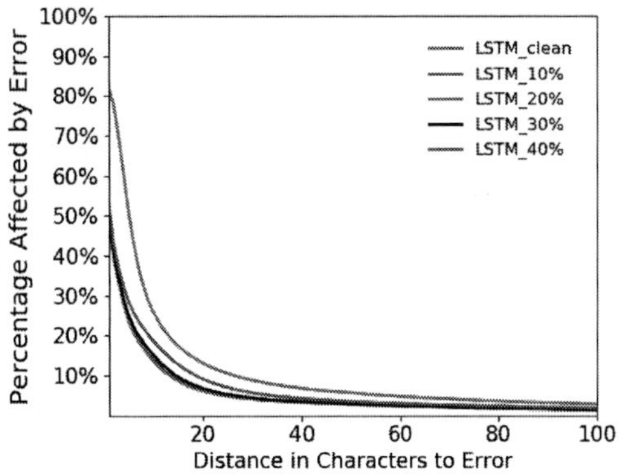

Figure 3: Percentage of predictions whose **MRR** is changed by an error, as a function of distance to the error: LSTM_clean is more sensitive for longer distance.

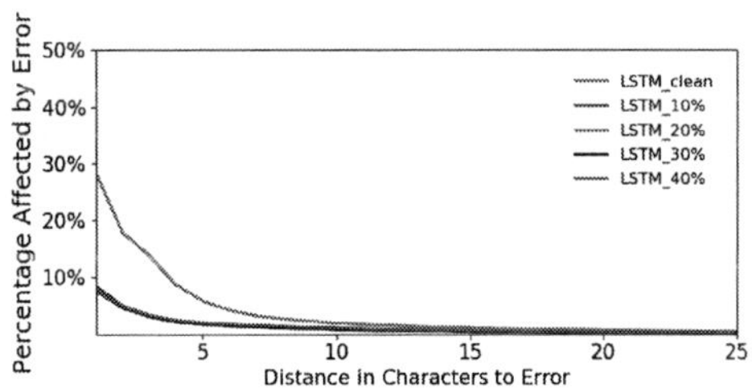

Figure 4: Percentage of predictions whose **recall** is changed by an error, as a function of distance to the error: LSTM_clean is more sensitive for longer distance.

4.3 How Do Errors Affect Nearby and Long-range Predictions?

Since recurrent LMs are sensitive to long-range contexts (Khandelwal et al., 2018), we investigate the impact of errors on the predictions following it. We inject an error into each character of each sentence in turn, and then examine how the LSTM models' predictive performance is affected by the distance to the error. Results are reported on the NYT corpus due to space. SUBTLEXus displays similar behavior.

Percentage of Predictions Affected Figures 3 and 4 show the percentage of predictions affected

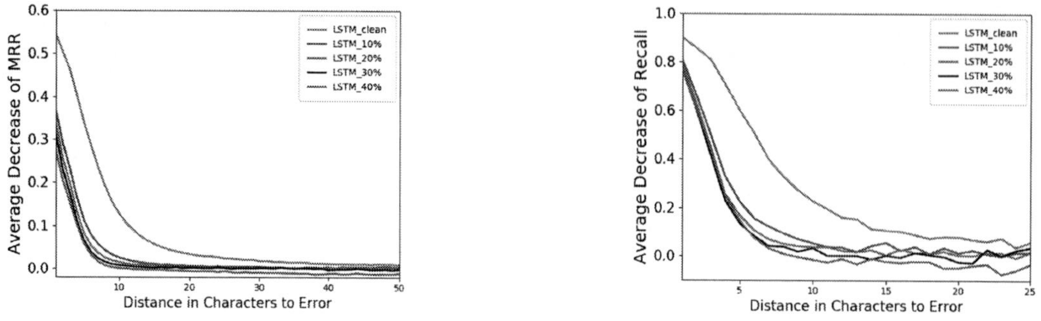

(a) MRR (b) Recall

Figure 5: Average decrease of performance at positions with different distances from the error for clean and noisy LSTM models

by the error at positions with different distance to the error: the closer to the error, the higher percentage of predictions affected. The impact of the error is higher and farther on LSTM_clean model than on the noisy models. The noisy models perform similarly, while the most noisy model (LSTM_40%) is slightly more influenced by the error. The error also affects MRR more significantly than Recall. For the noisy LSTMs, the MRR of more than 20% of prediction has been affected by the error within a five-character context, while the Recall of less than 10% of them has been affected. An error also has a longer-range effect on MRR than on Recall. An error affects the MRR of predictions about 40 characters after it, while it only affects the Recall of predictions about five characters after it. While the rank of the correct output among all the characters has been affected by the error, most are still in the top 10.

Performance Degradation Figure 5 presents the average degradation in performance for those predictions affected by the error. Again, we see that the farther away from the error, the smaller the degradation of performance could be observed. The drop of MRR and Recall is less significant about 10 characters after the error for the noisy LSTMs. It can also be observed that the average decrease of MRR and Recall fluctuate around 0 about 10 characters and 5 characters after the error, respectively. This is because the error affects the predictions of the noisy models farther than this distance more randomly and less significantly, i.e., it slightly increases the Recall and MRR of some predictions. This effect is most significant on LSTM_40%, which is trained with the most noisy data. The decrease of recall fluctuates after 5 characters, since the percentage of predictions whose recall is affected is much lower after this distance, as we could see from Figure 4.

4.4 Effect of Error at Different Positions within Words

Figure 6 presents the performance of LSTM models when seeing errors in different positions of the words. For each sentence, we randomly choose 20%, 30% and 40% of the words and corrupt each word at different positions: the first letter, the intermediate letters, the last letter, and the spaces after it. Since the character error rate is less than 10%, we test with LSTM_10%. We can see that when the data is noisier, the performance of the model is worse at all positions of the words. Furthermore, the impact of word error rate is most dramatic at the first letter, and the performance of the LSTM gets better when the error moves to later position in the word.

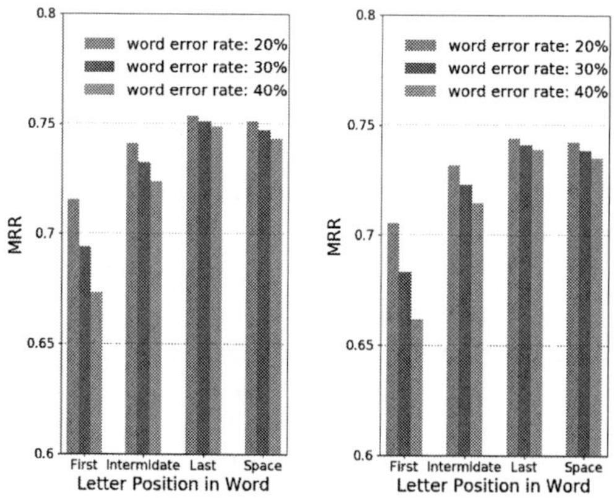

(a) NYT (b) Sublex

Figure 6: MRR of LSTM models tested on words with different noise rates at different positions.

4.5 Exploiting Ambiguous Histories

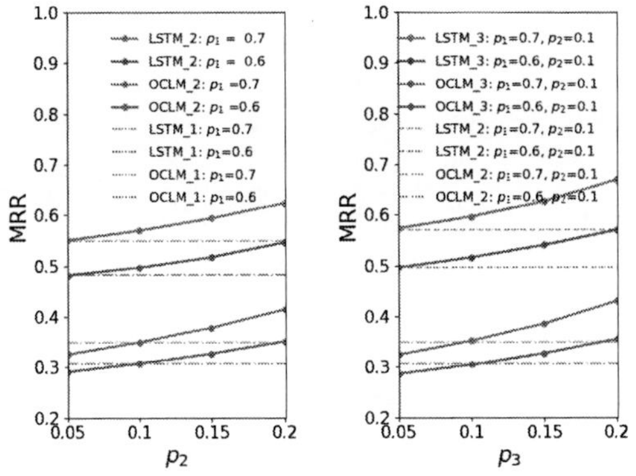

(a) 2 inputs (b) 3 inputs

Figure 7: Performance of LSTM and OCLM trained with 2 or 3 inputs compared to models trained with 1 less input .

Due to input noise, BCI systems might rank an erroneous character higher than the user's intended one. In this section, we explore whether incorporating ambiguous histories into the model could further improve the performance of neural language models on a simulated predictive typing task.

We simulate ambiguous histories by synthetically generating the top n candidate characters as well as their probabilities predicted by BCI systems at each time step. We ensure that adding one candidate will introduce 5% to 20% percent more correct characters to it. The Dirichlet distribution is used to sample a random multinomial distribution to assign the probabilities to the candidates.

A sum of the embeddings of candidate characters, weighted by those characters' probabilities, is then fed as input to the LSTM at each time step. Summing is much more efficient the OCLM or lattice encoder methods (Sperber et al., 2017). LSTM or OCLM models trained with n inputs are named LSTM_n or OCLM_n ($n \in \{1, 2, 3\}$). The correctness probability of characters in the kth candidate is p_k ($k \in \{1, 2, 3\}$). Performance is reported for LSTM and OCLM trained and tested on datasets with matched error rates.

We compare LSTM and OCLM models on randomly sampled 50K sentences from the test set for NYT corpus. This is because OCLM is slow due to the composition operations between finite state transducers. We find that LSTM performance with ambiguous history on the subset is consistent with its performance on the whole NYT test set as well as its performance on the SUBTLEXus test set reported above.

Figure 7 shows that both LSTM and OCLM work better when more correct characters are added into the inputs. We can see from Figure 7 that the MRR of LSTM has been increased by more than 13% percent when an extra candidate with 20% correctness probability is included; however, adding an extra candidate with 5% correctness probability does not significantly improve the performance of LSTM_2 model, compared to the determinstic model LSTM_1. It even causes a degradation in the performance of the OCLM, which means that the OCLM is more sensitive to the noise in the inputs.

Figure 7 also shows that when adding an input introduces enough correct characters, the performance of the model improves. Figure 7a shows that LSTM models trained with an ambiguous history of 2 inputs (LSTM_2) outperform LSTM models trained with deterministic history (LSTM_1), when the correct probability of the second candidate p_2 is more than 5%. Similar observation could be made for LSTM models with 3 inputs compared with those with 2 inputs in Figure 7b.

We can also see that the LSTM model significantly outperforms the OCLM on ambiguous histories. The OCLM has access to both word and character information, while the LSTM is trained on character sequences alone.

5 Conclusion

In this paper, we propose training language models on noisy text to improve their robustness on unseen noisy text. We also investigate the impact of errors in the history on the performance of recurrent language models. An efficient method of integrating ambiguous histories further improves model performance. We expect to experiment with more realistic error distributions as more real typing data becomes available.

Acknowledgments

We would like to thank the reviewers of the SLPAT workshop for their insightful comments and feedback. This work was supported by NIH grants 5R01DC009834-09 and 1R01DC015999-01. Any views, findings, conclusions, or recommendations expressed do not necessarily reflect those of the NIH.

References

Yonatan Belinkov and Yonatan Bisk. 2017. Synthetic and natural noise both break neural machine translation. *arXiv preprint arXiv:1711.02173*.

Marc Brysbaert and Boris New. 2009. Moving beyond Kučera and Francis: A critical evaluation of current word frequency norms and the introduction of a new and improved word frequency measure for American English. *Behavior Research Methods*, 41(4):977–990.

Shiran Dudy, Shaobin Xu, Steven Bedrick, and David Smith. 2018. A multi-context character prediction model for a brain-computer interface. In *Proceedings of the Second Workshop on Subword/Character LEvel Models*, pages 72–77.

Shaona Ghosh and Per Ola Kristensson. 2017. Neural networks for text correction and completion in keyboard decoding. *arXiv preprint arXiv:1709.06429*.

Kenneth Heafield. 2011. KenLM: Faster and smaller language model queries. In *Proc. Workshop on Statistical Machine Translation*, pages 187–197.

Sepp Hochreiter and Jürgen Schmidhuber. 1997. Long short-term memory. *Neural Computation*, 9(8):1735–1780.

Urvashi Khandelwal, He He, Peng Qi, and Dan Jurafsky. 2018. Sharp nearby, fuzzy far away: How neural language models use context. *arXiv preprint arXiv:1805.04623*.

Jun Li, Karim Ouazzane, Hassan B Kazemian, and Muhammad Sajid Afzal. 2013. Neural network approaches for noisy language modeling. *IEEE Transactions on Neural Networks and Learning Systems*, 24(11):1773–1784.

Anderson Mora-Cortes, Nikolay Manyakov, Nikolay Chumerin, and Marc Van Hulle. 2014. Language model applications to spelling with brain-computer interfaces. *Sensors*, 14(4):5967–5993.

Barry S. Oken, Umut Orhan, Brian Roark, Deniz Erdogmus, Andrew Fowler, Aimee Mooney, Betts Peters, Meghan Miller, and Melanie B. Fried-Oken. 2014. Brain-computer interface with language model–electroencephalography fusion for locked-in syndrome. *Neurorehabilitation and Neural Repair*, 28(4):387–394.

Evan Sandhaus. 2008. The New York Times annotated corpus. *Linguistic Data Consortium, Philadelphia*, 6(12):e26752.

Claude E. Shannon. 1951. Prediction and entropy of printed English. *Bell System Technical Journal*, 30(1).

William Speier, C. Arnold, and Nader Pouratian. 2016. Integrating language models into classifiers for BCI communication: A review. *Journal of Neural Engineering*, 13(3).

William Speier, Corey Arnold, Nand Chandravadia, Dustin Roberts, Shrita Pendekanti, and Nader Pouratian. 2018. Improving p300 spelling rate using language models and predictive spelling. *Brain-Computer Interfaces*, 5(1):13–22.

William Speier, Nand Chandravadia, Dustin Roberts, Shrita Pendekanti, and Nader Pouratian. 2017. Online BCI typing using language model classifiers by ALS patients in their homes. *Brain-Computer Interfaces*, 4(1-2):114–121.

Matthias Sperber, Graham Neubig, Jan Niehues, and Alex Waibel. 2017. Neural lattice-to-sequence models for uncertain inputs. In *EMNLP*.

Ziang Xie, Sida I Wang, Jiwei Li, Daniel Lévy, Aiming Nie, Dan Jurafsky, and Andrew Y Ng. 2017. Data noising as smoothing in neural network language models. *arXiv preprint arXiv:1703.02573*.

A Appendices

A.1 Effect of Error at Different Positions within Sentences

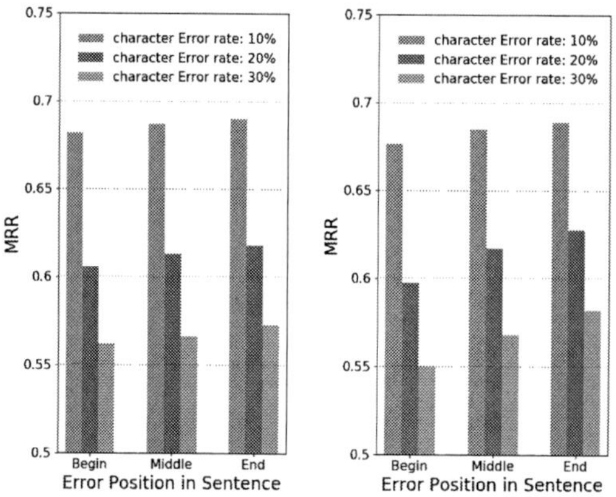

(a) NYT (b) Sublex

Figure 8: MRR of LSTM models tested on sentences with different noise rates at different positions.

We also investigate how the position of errors within sentences affects the predictive performance of LSTM models. Figure 8 shows the results of noisy LSTM models tested on sentences where errors appearing in beginning, middle, and end sections of a sentence. Each sentence is split into thirds, and an equal percentage of noise is added to each section in turn. Here, LSTM models are trained and tested on data with consistent noise rate. We can see that the performance of noisy LSTM models does not vary too much when the errors appear in different sections of the sentences. Errors appear at earlier positions in a sentence do not have a significant impact on the predictions in later positions in the sentence.

Author Index

Association for Computational Linguistics
209 N. Eighth Street
Stroudsburg, Pennsylvania 18360

ISBN 978-1-5108-8771-8

CURRAN ASSOCIATES INC.
proceedings.com